City Reborn

Kenneth Powell
Foreword by Renzo Piano

City Reborn

Architecture and Regeneration in London, from Bankside to Dulwich

MERRELL
LONDON · NEW YORK

First published 2004
by Merrell Publishers Limited

Head office:
42 Southwark Street
London SE1 1UN

New York office:
49 West 24th Street, 8th floor
New York, NY 10010

www.merrellpublishers.com

PUBLISHER Hugh Merrell
EDITORIAL DIRECTOR Julian Honer
US DIRECTOR Joan Brookbank
SALES AND MARKETING DIRECTOR Emilie Amos
SALES AND MARKETING EXECUTIVE Emily Sanders
MANAGING EDITOR Anthea Snow
EDITOR Sam Wythe
DESIGN MANAGER Nicola Bailey
PRODUCTION MANAGER Michelle Draycott
DESIGN AND PRODUCTION ASSISTANT Matt Packer

British Library Cataloguing-in-Publication Data:
City reborn : architecture and regeneration in London, from Bankside to
Dulwich
1.Buildings – England – London 2.Buildings – England – London – Pictorial
works 3.Architecture – England – London 4.Architecture – England –
London – Pictorial works 7.Southwark (London : England) – Buildings,
structures, etc. 8.Southwark (London : England) – Buildings, structures,
etc. – Pictorial works
I.Title
720.9'42164

ISBN 1 85894 269 1

Produced by Merrell Publishers Limited
Project-managed on behalf of London Borough of Southwark
by Will Reading
Designed by Claudia Schenk
Editorial management by Iona Baird and Anthea Snow
Copy-edited by Ian McDonald

Printed and bound in China

Jacket front: Millennium Bridge, Foster and Partners,
1996–2001; see pp. 78–79
Jacket back: City Hall, Foster and Partners,
1998–2002; see pp. 92–93

Southwark Council actively encourages high-quality architecture and
urban design as a principal catalyst for social and economic renewal in
the borough. The council was voted local authority of the year in 2002
by CABE and the RIBA, and regularly features in *RIBA Journal*'s annual
top fifty clients list.

ontents

Bob Coomber
Chief Executive, London Borough of Southwark

Southwark Council has a clear vision – to make the borough a high-quality place for those who live or work here and for those who are drawn to visit it. That vision drives the way we deliver services in the borough, working with our many public and private partners. It derives from a wide engagement with local people.

The borough has an outstanding history and physical heritage. Kenneth Powell summarizes these in his introductory essay. But Southwark has always been a dynamic and changing place. This book shows how, over the last two decades, the council has been at the forefront of supporting and managing that change – for the benefit of London and for the benefit of local people.

The buildings illustrated here are just a selection of the best that has been achieved. Some are recognized as being world class – Peckham Library won the Stirling Prize in 2000. All have contributed hugely to improving the quality of life. Many illustrate innovative solutions to the changing demands of urban living.

Almost all of the schemes are completed; they represent practical achievement, often transforming the area within which they sit – evident most notably in the impact of Tate Modern coming to the borough. A few of them illustrate the extent of our continuing ambition, as evidenced by our strong support for the 'Shard of Glass'.

We commissioned this record, with support from many partners, to demonstrate and celebrate the achievements made so far, and to stimulate everyone to participate in widening and strengthening the commitment to achieving quality in the design of the built environment.

As a council we are proud to have been an enlightened patron – we have been asked whether we see ourselves as 'the new Medici'. Perhaps that is a little too grand a concept – and no one has offered the chief executive a palace!

There is nevertheless an honourable tradition of leadership and patronage from public bodies. We will demonstrate how that role can be developed. We will use the practical direct action of commissioning buildings ourselves and of driving forward regeneration projects. We will set out planning policies that encourage quality; and we will use our influence as a community leader to stimulate others to achieve quality as well. That benchmark of quality will apply not only to the larger buildings that make up much of this book but also to the many smaller buildings that constitute the fabric of our changing city. It will also apply to the public realm, which has to be well designed and maintained.

In the next decade I believe Southwark will see further achievements to match those illustrated here. We will be a leader in the continuing revival of London, and in its growth as a world city, while always improving the quality of life for those who live here.

Bob Allies and Graham Morrison, Allies & Morrison Architects

Southwark is a place for architectural invention. Although the borough has a strong and unique history, it does not suffer from the overbearing pomposity of some other quarters of our city. It has always been a place where work gets *done*, as demonstrated by the many pub names that reflect its colourful old trades: the Mudlarker, the Market Porter and the Mad Hatter. Southwark used to supply London with many of its needs.

The borough's street pattern, derived from layers of energetic use, is a rich network that reveals its historic vigour and spontaneity. The result of this dynamic history is a copious variety of city blocks, each characterized by a shape and scale that carries the memory of earlier activity.

Southwark is straightforward and direct, but it is also surprising and powerful. Its future is based on an inheritance that is both stimulating and provocative – it will demand much from twenty-first-century designers.

There is an air of expectation and optimism here, a sense that Southwark is a place where creativity will thrive – something that we can speak of personally, on behalf of our own architectural practice. When we moved from the West End to Southwark in 2003, we brought with us 170 architects and other members of staff, many of whom now live in the borough. Our thoughts had been focused on Southwark for some time, not only in the intention to acquire a site for our own use in Southwark Street, and to design a building for ourselves that would express our beliefs as architects, but also, as part of that credo, to integrate our building with the fabric of its south London urban context.

London is our city, but Southwark is our home. Our biggest current project is right in front of us: Bankside 123, over a million square feet (100,000 square metres) of office space. Our plans provide for new streets with much-needed shops, and new vistas to Tate Modern and the Thames. It is a place that we ourselves shall use along with our neighbours. It will give us great pleasure to watch these plans come to reality, literally before our eyes.

An architect's plans are only as effective as the relationship with the immediate community and its planning authority. Allies & Morrison has found that this borough is one in which it is possible to build and develop. There is forward-thinking here, and there are open minds. It is a fertile environment for any team, whether the focus is business, creativity or both.

Acknowledgements

The London Borough of Southwark would like to express its thanks to the following organizations, who have supported this project through sponsorship. Without their generous support, this publication would not have been possible.

Land Securities
More London Development Ltd
DP9
Sellars
Foster and Partners

The London Borough of Southwark would like to thank the following people for their contributions to this unique project. First, Liam Bond, Paul Henry, Julian Honer and Graham Morrison, for their encouragement and support in the earliest stages, and for their continued assistance and advice; also Piers Gough, whose enthusiasm for this borough, and for this book, has been a great help to us.

We should like to thank all of the architectural practices and their staff, and the many private individuals, who have contributed to this project through supplying images and information, without which this project would not have been realized.

Thank you also to the Urban Design and Conservation Team at Southwark Council, for their patience, understanding and help over the last year.

Finally, we should like to thank Kenneth Powell, for enabling this project, and for his knowledge, enthusiasm and commitment to our work and our borough.

My thanks to the members and officers of Southwark Council for commissioning this record of a remarkable two decades of change and regeneration in the borough. In particular, I am grateful to Julie Greer, who came up with the idea for this book, to Paul Evans for supporting the project and making it possible, and to Will Reading, whose labours, including the gathering of pictures and information, were fundamental to its success.

At Merrell Publishers, with its offices close to the heart of historic Southwark, Julian Honer took up the idea of the book with his usual enthusiasm; Iona Baird and Anthea Snow were painstaking managing editors; and Claudia Schenk demonstrated an unerring eye in her design of the layouts.

Finally, thanks are due to the architects, owners and managers of the buildings featured, who arranged access, gave freely of their time and, in some cases, offered valued sponsorship. Inspired designers need inspired clients and Southwark has more than its share of both.

Kenneth Powell
London 2004

Foreword

Foreword

Renzo Piano

Southwark is one of those places where you can feel the layers of history: you can tell how the city has grown organically from the morphology of nature, the topography of the ground and the curve of the river.

The fact is that Southwark was never actually designed: it has simply grown out of millions of single true lives. And of these lives it is a faithful mirror.

When people ask me what the city of the future will be like, my answer is: it will be like that of the past, I hope – so rich, so complex, so surprising and so unpredictable.

Southwark looks so attractive and fascinating with its crowded streets and small piazzas, with its unexpected stairways and colourful markets, and with its sudden views on to the river. But it has now to confront all those problems affecting a modern city: traffic, public safety, transparency and quality of life.

Little by little, the railway has been building an insurmountable barrier right in the heart of the neighbourhood. St Thomas Street has been cut off from Tooley Street by gloomy and sinister underpasses – true kingdoms of darkness.

Is it possible to solve these problems without betraying the identity of these places? I think so. And, in my view, the project for London Bridge Tower aims to do this.

It is not hermetic and mysterious, nor is it alien to the city. It is instead a small vertical town with many functions, most of which are public, that allow the site to live around the clock. Furthermore, the urban logic that organizes the entire project is one of public transport. There is no parking beneath the tower. People have to use the train, the Underground and the bus to commute.

London Bridge Tower, this thin and light tower, a real shard of glass, will eventually put Southwark on the map of London: it is a symbol, but does not strive to become one.

Sketch by Renzo Piano of London Bridge Tower, the so-called 'Shard of Glass', a proposed new scheme for London Bridge station.

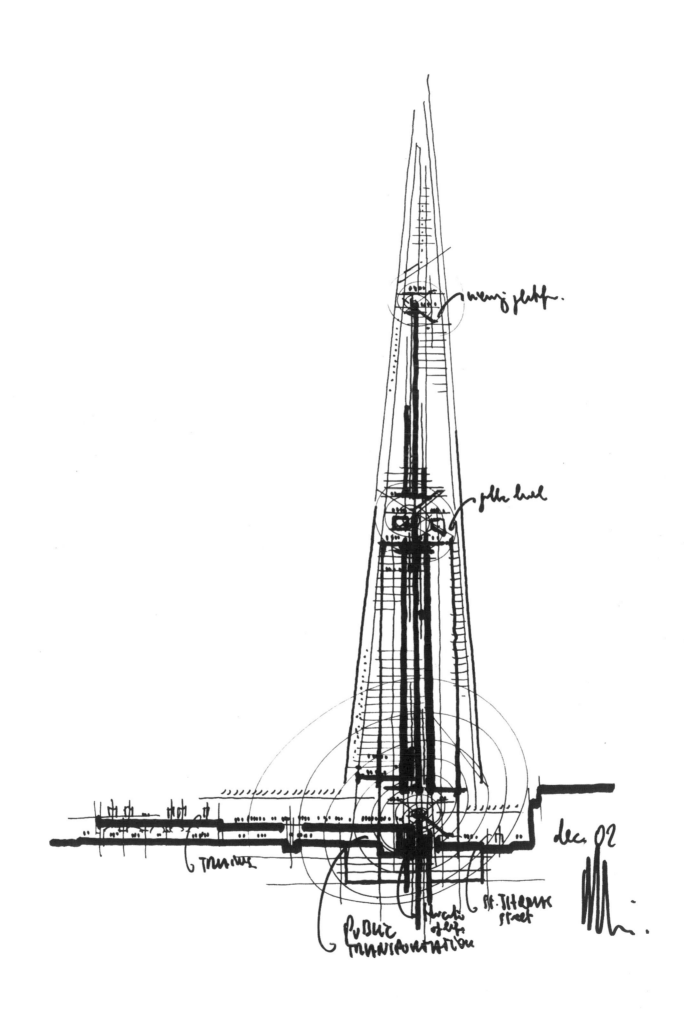

wenij plotifi

jehle hivel

dec 02

Transition

Public
Transportation

St. Thomas
Street

Introduction

Southwark: Medieval to Modern
Kenneth Powell

"More intimately London than any other area outside the City and Westminster", wrote Sir Nikolaus Pevsner, the great chronicler of British architecture, about Southwark. He was referring, of course, to the ancient core of Southwark, the 'Borough', close to London Bridge, that had developed as a suburb of the city in Roman times. Though it was for centuries formally under the control of the city authorities, the area around Bankside and Borough High Street was a place where activities considered unseemly on the north bank of the Thames (bear baiting, theatres and brothels, for example, as well as hospitals for those sick in mind or body) positively thrived. One of the twenty-three inns along Borough High Street was the point of departure for Chaucer's pilgrims, and Southwark was the chosen location for the mansions of church dignitaries – only a fragment of one of them, Winchester House, survives today. At its heart was a substantial monastery, the priory of St Mary Overie founded in the twelfth century, its church – the rest has long vanished – now Southwark Cathedral. There were seven prisons, including the Clink and the Marshalsea (where Charles Dickens's father was locked up for debt) and, by the late eighteenth century, some of the worst slums in London were close at hand. The area around Jacob's Island in Bermondsey was referred to in 1849 as "the very capital of cholera". Three-quarters of a century later, the writer V.S. Pritchett, who as a young man worked in the leather industry, recalled streets in the same area that smelt variously of hops, boots, dog dung and vinegar, all of them overhung with smoke and with "the sharp stink of poverty".

Modern Southwark extends far beyond Bankside, forming a triangle of territory contained between Surrey Quays (formerly the Surrey Docks) and the hinterland of Waterloo to the north and the leafy heights of Dulwich at its southern tip. The present-day borough dates only from 1965, when the existing boroughs of Southwark, Bermondsey and Camberwell (themselves late Victorian in origin) were merged. As a slice of urban (and suburban) terrain, Southwark is remarkably varied, physically, socially and culturally. The ancient bridgehead core apart, it is largely a creation of the eighteenth and nineteenth centuries. During this period Bermondsey and Rotherhithe became a continuous expanse of wharves and warehouses, with the 105 ha (460 acres) of the Surrey Commercial Docks being developed between the 1800s and the 1920s, principally as a centre for the import of timber. (By the mid-1870s, the Surreys were handling over 600,000 tonnes of timber annually – 80% of that coming into London by sea.) The population of the old boroughs of Southwark and Bermondsey grew from around 100,000 in 1801 to nearly 240,000 a century later, while the fields around formerly rustic villages such as Nunhead and Peckham Rye were steadily filled with houses and connected by suburban railways – London's first rail line terminated at London Bridge.

Beginning in the mid-1960s, the rapid closure of London's docks, from the Pool of London to the Royals (the Royal Victoria, Royal Albert and King George V docks, near Beckton), hit Southwark hard. A staggering total of 150,000 jobs were lost over little more than a decade (the docks had enjoyed a boom during the 1950s). This was followed by the steady decline of traditional industries – many of them, such as food processing, linked to the import trade. But the post-war landscape of Southwark was transformed even more radically by the housing-renewal programme that had begun in earnest in the 1920s and 1930s, but which accelerated dramatically after the Second World War – by 1977 nearly two-thirds of all the homes in the borough were council-owned. Sadly, much of the new housing consisted of what Pevsner described as "the impersonal megalomaniac creations of the mid C20 … notorious products of industrialized building" – the Heygate and Aylesbury estates, together housing around 12,000 people, fully justify this description. The then-fashionable strategy of segregating vehicles and people was rigidly applied in these projects, with people banished to 'streets in the sky'. (A typically 'visionary' device at Heygate was to build roads without pavements on the assumption that people would use the upper-level connections – today everyone walks in the road.) The Elephant & Castle redevelopment, begun in 1956, relegated pedestrians to tunnels beneath the dominant road system. The architecture of its new shopping centre was almost irrelevant in the face of such a hostile urban environment. The mid-1960s saw a fine group of historic houses (where Lord Snowdon had been a resident) in Rotherhithe demolished, as part of a clearance campaign – which continued into the 1970s – that turned the eastern part of Jamaica Road almost into a motorway.

The Modern Movement had first made its impact in Southwark during the 1930s. St Olave House, off Tooley Street, completed in 1932 for the Hay's Wharf Corporation and well restored in the 1980s, might best be described as "modernistic". Its architect, H.S. Goodhart-Rendel (also responsible for Holy Trinity Church on Jamaica Road some thirty years later), combined a modern concrete structure and orthogonal form with decoration, internal and external, of a broadly Art Deco character. In contrast, 'Six Pillars' in Dulwich, designed by Berthold Lubetkin's young partner Valentine Harding and completed in 1935, is a classic 'White Modern' house, built for an affluent client and recently carefully restored by John Winter. Maxwell Fry's Sassoon House in Peckham (1932) was a pioneering exercise in Modernist mass

A panorama of Southwark's riverside (pages 12–13), a dynamic mix of the historic and the modern, including Renzo Piano's proposed London Bridge Tower. The Southwark we have lost: a view of Sumner Street (opposite), close to Blackfriars Bridge, in 1912. The streetscape in this picture has now vanished.

housing. More significant in terms of its social impact, however, was the nearby Pioneer Health Centre, designed by the great architect–engineer Owen Williams for a group of progressive doctors who wanted to promote healthy ways of living, as well as to give poor families access to medical treatment. With its swimming pool, gym, crèche and social facilities, the centre's agenda was extremely forward-looking (and was echoed, for example, in the recent Peckham Pulse – see pp. 64–65). Some judged the industrial aesthetic of the building (opened in 1935) a little severe, though J.M. Richards, writing in the *Architectural Review*, admired it as "a piece of machinery". Subsequently, under the National Health Service, the ideas behind it were lost and, more recently, the building – which predated Lubetkin's better-known Finsbury Health Centre – has been disposed of for alternative use.

Clearing the slums, an imperative from the late nineteenth century into the post-1945 era, meant providing alternative accommodation for their inhabitants, often in new suburban housing estates far from the inner city. (The population

of Bermondsey in 1951 was less than half that recorded fifty years earlier.) Wilson Grove, developed in the 1920s, is a surprising slice of low-rise Garden City in the heart of Bermondsey, built under the inspiration of the pioneering local doctor Alfred Salter. In general, however, the new housing took the form of flats. Even after the war, the typical 1930s 'balcony flat' continued to be built, basically neo-Georgian in style and brick-faced. Many blocks of this type remain in use and a number have been successfully renovated. But both the local authority (or, pre-1965, authorities) and the London County Council (LCC) were increasingly wedded to Modernism. The Brandon Estate, designed by Edward Hollamby of the LCC Architects' Department, is unquestionably the most successful of the large-scale post-war housing schemes. Noting the crop of new high-rise commercial buildings beginning to transform London's skyline, *The Architects' Journal* judged the estate "the Welfare State's first major addition to the new power symbols of the Metropolis", its towers "identifying Southwark and giving the lost motorist his bearings for the first time in the brick jungle of south London". Although it was the towers (initially six, of eighteen storeys, completed in 1958 – with five more of twenty-six storeys each added, less successfully, in the 1960s) that made the estate such a visual landmark, its real innovation lay in the decision to retain and modernize 182 existing terraced houses earmarked for clearance. This move was a milestone, indeed, in housing philosophy. The Brandon Estate remains a classic of its time.

While local authority teams and the LCC architects dominated the post-war housing scene, some of the most innovative ideas came from private sector practices. The Setchell Estate in Bermondsey, designed by Neylan & Ungless and constructed between 1972 and

1978, aimed at a village character, with low-rise housing around traditional streets. Peter Moro was responsible for a number of residential infill developments of the late 1960s and 1970s that respected an existing context – an increasingly valued commodity as the appeal of the Modernist utopia began to fade. Other major practitioners were brought in to work on schools: Chamberlin, Powell & Bon for the extraordinary Geoffrey Chaucer School near the Elephant & Castle, and Stirling and Gowan for Brunswick Park School, Camberwell – praised by the critic Ian Nairn for its "consistent waywardness". Ernö Goldfinger's Alexander Fleming House, begun in 1959 as offices for the then Ministry of Health, gave some dignity to the reconstructed Elephant & Castle. A highly individual work, inspired by Goldfinger's great mentor Auguste Perret, it was seriously threatened with demolition before being sold to a developer and converted (with, sadly, little respect for the quality of the architecture) to apartments. Goldfinger's fine Odeon Cinema adjoining it was needlessly destroyed while the fate of the whole complex was in limbo.

By the later 1960s the property boom that had transformed swathes of the City and West End began to have an impact on London south of the river, with major office developments adjacent to London Bridge station and at King's Reach, next to Blackfriars Bridge, where Richard Seifert's stumpy tower dominates the riverside. These developments offered little to the local community in terms of amenity or employment. The response of the local authority to the decline of the docks and other traditional industries was understandably defensive, and it generally resisted the redevelopment of industrial buildings and sites for other uses. By the early 1980s, however, offices had colonized the area around Hay's Wharf adjacent to London Bridge, where London Bridge City was developed to a 1982

Hay's Galleria (above) was formed in the early 1980s by draining and covering over Hay's Dock (opposite).

Long threatened with demolition, the Oxo building with its famous tower was later converted to affordable housing, workshops, retail spaces and restaurants.

masterplan by Twigg Brown, with buildings by this firm and The John S. Bonnington Partnership. The new architecture was unexciting, but at least some of the existing structures were retained and Hay's Dock (where the first New Zealand butter had reached Britain in the 1860s) was infilled – with a covering that is, in theory, removable – and roofed over to form Hay's Galleria (see pp. 34–35). The latter, if hardly a truly public space, offered some degree of community gain, and continues to be heavily used by tourists and by people working locally. The extent of anti-developer feeling in London, however, at a time when the Thatcher government was promoting a strongly pro-enterprise agenda, was evident just across the borough boundary in Lambeth, where Richard Rogers's Coin Street project was derailed by opposition from community activists and the Greater London Council in 1984. (The Oxo Tower project – see pp. 68–69 – was later developed on part of the site by Coin Street Community Builders, which became an enlightened client in its own right.)

During the 1970s, with the development industry in recession, community and conservation became powers to be reckoned with in London: the age of comprehensive redevelopment seemed to be over, and Modernist ideals in architecture and planning were widely scorned. In Southwark, however, the legacy of the industrial past posed a dilemma, as the fact that the old industries would never return sank in. Shad Thames, which had been a lively working area a couple of decades earlier, was sliding into picturesque decrepitude – a wonderful location for film-makers, but the prospect of mass demolitions loomed. In 1982, consent was given, after a public inquiry, to demolish the listed St Mary Overie Wharf, a very fine warehouse of the 1880s, thereby completing a clean sweep of old dock buildings in the vicinity. Other fine

warehouses were torn down with indecent haste before they could be listed, or succumbed to unfortunate fires. Big developers, backed by financial institutions and experienced in large-scale new-build projects, saw little prospect of profit in conversion schemes.

Against this backcloth, a new breed of entrepreneurs seized the opportunity offered by convertible old buildings. Andrew Wadsworth, then in his early twenties, was one of these pioneers. Discovering the warehouses of New Concordia Wharf, Wadsworth, whose business interests included restoring vintage Bentleys, enquired whether he might buy part of the complex to build his own loft-style apartment there. He ended up buying the entire building. Working initially with architect Nicholas Lacey, another Docklands pioneer – the term 'Docklands' was coined in the 1970s – and subsequently with Pollard Thomas Edwards architects, Wadsworth won consent from Southwark Council to convert the building to apartments (see pp. 30–31). The decision was something of a watershed for the local authority, but later in 1981 the London Docklands Development Corporation (LDDC) was given planning powers over all the borough's dockland territory, a wedge of land contained by Tooley Street, Jamaica Road and Lower Road. The brief from the Tory government was to promote development, by attracting new residents and new businesses to the area and streamlining the planning process. The disempowered local councils, all Labour-controlled, naturally protested but were powerless. Canary Wharf on the Isle of Dogs, developed from 1987 as an international business zone, was seen as the supreme expression of the LDDC's policies. In fact, in Southwark, as elsewhere in Docklands, the LDDC's term of office (the corporation was wound up in 1998) saw a sea-change in attitudes. The idea of regeneration, with the

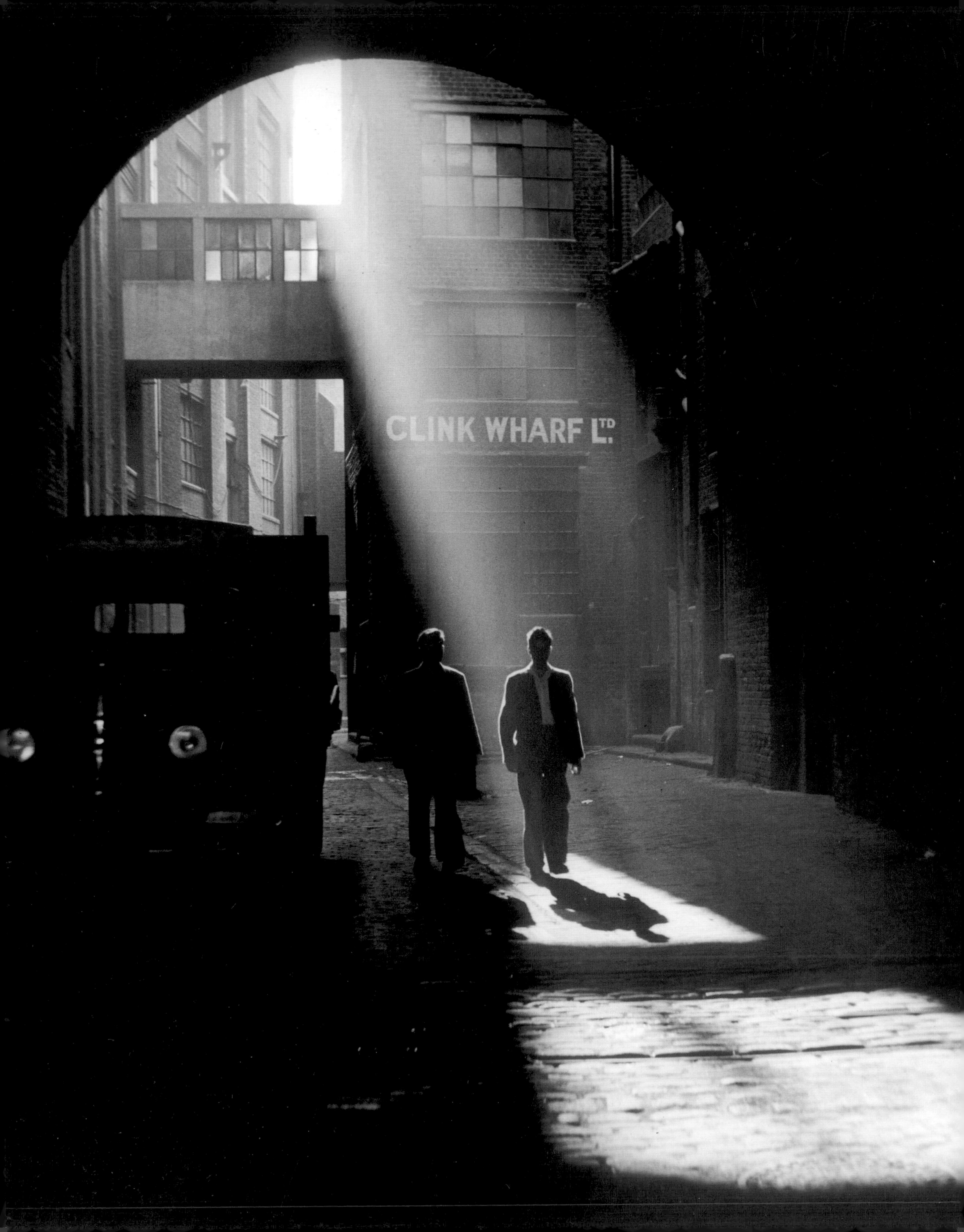
CLINK WHARF LTD

need to create new businesses and sources of employment in areas decimated by industrial change, was steadily accepted across the political spectrum. (With its interventionist brief and use of public funds for infrastructure improvements, the LDDC itself posed a challenge to free market Thatcherite doctrines.) Increasingly, the need for a regeneration strategy that clearly benefited the whole community – the incoming 'yuppie' was an unpopular figure – was taken on board.

Architecturally, the 1980s are remembered as the high point of Postmodernism. One of the movement's key figures, Piers Gough of CZWG, was brought in by Andrew Wadsworth to design China Wharf – a building that the historian of Postmodernism, Charles Jencks, deems "canonic" and an antidote to the ubiquitous "wharfism" of Docklands (see pp. 36–37). Southwark, indeed, became a regular stamping ground for CZWG, with the Circle at Butler's Wharf, Bankside Lofts for the Manhattan Loft Corporation (see pp. 46–47 and 74–75), and other built schemes at Rotherhithe, Surrey Quays, Southwark Street and, most recently, Clink Street. Piers Gough, whose work is sufficiently challenging to raise planning eyebrows on occasions, sees Southwark as an "inspirational" place – "it challenges you to contribute something worthwhile", he says, paying tribute to the increasingly encouraging approach of the local authority towards new development in this period. The Victorian engineer Sir Joseph Bazalgette, the creator of London's system of sewers and of the series of embankments along the north bank of the Thames from Chelsea to Blackfriars, was keen to open up the south bank in a similar way, but the entrenched interests of the wharf and warehouse owners proved an insuperable obstacle. In the late twentieth century, the survival of the dense and apparently unplanned townscape of Rotherhithe and Bermondsey –

equally resistant to post-war reconstruction – proved an asset for Southwark; it was ideal terrain for colonization by lofts, restaurants and bars while the City sacrificed its riverside to roads and office blocks. As the old industries continued to fade away, a steady supply of convertible buildings became available. The Courage Brewery on Shad Thames, for example, with its origins in the eighteenth century, closed in 1982. Much of it was cleared for Julyan Wickham's excellent Horselydown Square development (see pp. 42–43) – but the most striking of its buildings, the Anchor Brewhouse on the riverside, was converted to sixty-two apartments by Pollard Thomas Edwards architects. The scheme formed one element in the redevelopment of the area around Butler's Wharf, in which designer and entrepreneur Sir Terence Conran played a key role, not least in establishing the Design Museum (see pp. 44–45) there. Conran's own architectural practice, Conran Roche, along with Michael Hopkins, CZWG, Julyan Wickham, and Allies & Morrison, contributed to the creation of an area where good new architecture and intelligent reuse in sensitive balance provided a model, not only for the rest of Docklands, but equally for similar industrial quarters across Britain. As the property market boomed again in the 1990s, redundant industrial buildings well removed from the riverside were recast as housing. Wallis Gilbert's Alaska Factory in Grange Road (converted by ORMS for London Buildings) and the former Hartley's Jam Factory off Tower Bridge Road (Ian Simpson Architects for Angel Property) are recent examples.

Jencks's comments on "wharfism" highlighted the issue of style in new Docklands architecture. Conran Roche favoured a straightforward Functionalist aesthetic. The Prince's Tower apartment block on Rotherhithe Street, designed by Troughton McAslan and completed

Clink Wharf (opposite), an atmospheric view of a typical Docklands street before the decline of the Port of London, and new plans for Clink Street by Edward Cullinan Architects (top).

in 1990, eschewed local traditions in favour of a revived seaside 'White Modern' look inspired, perhaps, by Mendelsohn and Chermayeff's De La Warr Pavilion in Bexhill-on-Sea of 1935. (The building suffered from poor detailing – faceted rather than curved glass, for instance, in the fenestration of the bowed façade.) New building in the Surrey Docks reflected land and property values considerably lower than those in the more accessible parts of Docklands – before the Jubilee Line Extension (JLE) was built, the 'Surreys' suffered from poor transport links to central London. Because of the nature of their trade, they lacked the imposing multi-storey warehouses typical of Bermondsey and Rotherhithe, and most of the buildings were demolished after the docks closed – the Surrey Commercial Docks ceased operations as far back as 1969.

The 'Surreys' provided the opportunity to create what would be virtually a new town within the city, on a cleared site. The lack of an imaginative masterplan for the area was reflected, however, in the infilling of the majority of the docks during the early 1970s by the local authority (which had acquired most of the land from the Port of London Authority). The subsequent development of the area was characterized by what Pevsner's *Buildings of England* describes as "wide semi-rural vistas and pockets of exhibitionist housing", alongside more mundane local-authority residential schemes. A flashy shopping centre and a sprawl of retail sheds and printing plants contributed little to the local scene. A change of direction under the LDDC saw some expanses of water, notably the Greenland Dock, retained. Around this dock, a series of 1980s housing developments capitalize, with varying degrees of success, on the waterside setting – those by Shepheard Epstein & Hunter and by the Danish practice of Kjaer & Richter are the most successful, not least for their appropriate scale.

The rundown and abolition (in 1998) of the LDDC coincided with an increased emphasis on regeneration within the local authority. Fred Manson, a long-serving and charismatic planner who contributed much to the current development scene in Southwark, was appointed Director of Regeneration and Environment (the post's title is significant) in 1994. This was the year in which the Tate Gallery announced that the former Bankside Power Station would be the location for its new museum of modern art (subsequently Tate Modern – see pp. 66–67) and launched a competition to select an architect for the adaptation of the building, the choice finally falling on Herzog & de Meuron.

This was also the year in which the National Lottery, which John Major's government had decided to establish two years earlier, began its operations. It was to be a key source of funding not only for Tate Modern, via the Millennium Commission, but also for a number of other regenerative projects in Southwark. After a decade or more of planning, Dulwich Picture Gallery (see pp. 72–73), for example, was finally able to equip itself as a modern museum, and to restore and reinstate Soane's famous galleries. Another landmark decision by the Major administration was to give the green light to the JLE, a project with its origins (as the Fleet line) back in the 1960s. The route of the line extended through Southwark from Waterloo to the Surrey Docks via London Bridge, and included three entirely new stations at Bermondsey, Canada Water and Southwark (see pp. 54–55, 56–57 and 58–59); that at Canada Water ended the long isolation of the Surrey Docks. The JLE was significant not only as infrastructure, and as heroic engineering through difficult terrain, but equally for its inspirational approach to commissioning architects. Southwark Council has taken on board the message that good architecture and urban design are fundamental

Pictured here in 1947, the former brewhouse on the river (opposite) was the only part of the Courage Brewery complex retained in the redevelopment of the Butler's Wharf area. City Hall, the Dulwich Picture Gallery and London Bridge station (from top) are all symbols of the regeneration of Southwark.

to regeneration in its masterplan for the so-called Bermondsey Spa quarter (see pp. 110–11) behind Jamaica Road, a short walk from the JLE station. More than 2000 new homes, plus shops and health and recreation facilities, are promised as part of a project that involves such architectural practices as Lifschutz Davidson, Pollard Thomas Edwards architects and IDOM UK.

The need for regeneration in Southwark remained urgent. In 2003 it was reckoned that the borough ranked number nine among the most deprived urban areas in England, with a rate of unemployment twice the national average. While a front-rank cultural project such as Tate Modern could have an enormous impact in attracting visitors and businesses to the surrounding area, there was also a need to encourage commercial development. After the recession of the early 1990s, the City of London, across the Thames, was booming, but increasingly searching for the space for large business developments that had been found so easily in the Isle of Dogs. The City's connections with 'the Borough' went back 2000 years, so that Southwark provided a natural location in which City businesses could expand. There had long been plans for a second phase of London Bridge City and in 1988 a series of proposals for the site were exhibited, including a 'Venice on Thames' scheme by classicist John Simpson. The 1990s recession put the site into limbo for a decade, and by 1998 it had found new owners and become the subject of a new masterplan by Foster and Partners. Undoubtedly fuelled by the arrival of the JLE, the development got off the ground quickly and the decision by Tony Blair's government to site the headquarters of the Mayor of London and London Assembly (see pp. 92–93) there gave it added cachet. The success of More London (see pp. 94–95) doubtless encouraged developer British Land to proceed with a very large office scheme (Bankside 123 – see pp. 118–19) on the site of St Christopher's

House, a vast and particularly ugly 1950s government office block on Southwark Street, close to Tate Modern. Both projects offer considerable gains in terms of public space: More London provides through routes from London Bridge station and Tooley Street to the river, while Bankside 123 opens up the hinterland of the Tate. In 2003 Southwark Council expressed strong support for the 306 m (1016 ft) high London Bridge Tower designed by Renzo Piano and subsequently approved by the government after a public inquiry (see pp. 114–15). The sky, it was clear, was the limit to Southwark's regenerative ambitions – the building, it was argued, would be a marker of urban renaissance. In his evidence to the public inquiry, Director of Regeneration Paul Evans insisted that the project was fundamental to a vision of the borough as both dynamic and extremely attractive to live in.

The regeneration projects of the 1990s, however, were not restricted to the northern, riverside edge of the borough. At the centre of Peckham, the council commissioned Will Alsop, then rapidly taking his place in the front rank of British architects, to design a different sort of public library as the centrepiece for a new civic hub around Peckham Square (see pp. 88–89). The building went on to win the RIBA's Stirling Prize. And regeneration was not only about new buildings. The transformation, under the aegis of a council project, of the Bellenden area of Peckham, an established enclave of Victorian housing, highlighted the role of art in urban transformation – it was fortuitous, perhaps, that one local resident was sculptor Antony Gormley.

It was ironic that while much nineteenth-century housing still functioned well and was considered 'desirable', the brave housing experiments of the post-war era had often become distinctly undesirable places to live. The Aylesbury Estate, completed as recently as 1977, has become the subject of a major transformation

project under the government's Communities for Change scheme. Another housing scheme of the same period, the Heygate Estate, faces demolition as part of the development framework for the Elephant & Castle area adopted by Southwark Council in 2004. It is intended to provide 4200 new homes and as many new jobs, re-establishing the Elephant as 'the Piccadilly Circus of South London'. (Before the Second World War, this was a place of shops, music halls and pubs, where south Londoners went for a night out.) While a previous masterplan for the area, which did not command the support of local residents, focused on the development of a large enclosed retail centre, the new framework is essentially about a public realm around new buildings – a civic square will replace the existing traffic roundabout and there will be a major park. Above all, the vision is one in which streets are for people: a complete contrast to the Elephant as it now exists. The project exemplifies the genuine public/private partnership route that Southwark now sees as crucial to regeneration.

The process of regeneration extends across the whole borough, but Southwark's true heart remains its ancient core, close to London Bridge. Southwark Cathedral was long a proverbial 'hidden gem' of London, undervalued as a work of medieval architecture and little visited by tourists. Richard Griffiths's Millennium Project has given the cathedral both the practical facilities and the dignified setting that it lacked (see pp. 84–85). Close by is another classic example of both continuity and renewal. Borough Market is an institution that is probably older even than Southwark Cathedral, in that its origins lie in the medieval markets held in the nearby High Street. Until the mid-1990s it was a wholesale market in slow decline, set perhaps to go the way of Covent Garden and Spitalfields in the course of time. By 1998 a speciality retail market was operating there on one Saturday a month. Now it operates two days every week and has become a popular London institution (see pp. 86–87). The ongoing renovation and extension of the market received funding from Southwark's own Conservation Area Partnership and (with government backing) from the Single Regeneration Budget for London. The market is a magnet for 'foodies', with a growing selection of cafes, pubs and restaurants surrounding it, but it is also the catalyst for a mixed-use renewal of the surrounding area, with small craft-based industries colonizing vacant local space. The inspired decision to site a new entrance to London Bridge Underground station directly opposite the market helped, of course, and forms the starting-point for a pedestrian network extending via the Globe Theatre to Tate Modern. "From the new Tate Modern to the Globe and then to the Anchor public house, the broad walkway is commonly filled with people", wrote Peter Ackroyd in 2000. "The ancient hospitality and freedom of the South are emerging once more; in the twenty-first century it will become one of the most vigorous and varied, not to say popular, centres of London life."

At the beginning of the twenty-first century Southwark is certainly vigorous and varied, its social and economic renaissance reflected in some of London's best new architecture. More significant, however, than the quality of individual buildings is the way in which they contribute to a rich, increasingly enjoyable and accessible public domain. Landmarks count for much, but the challenge for architects working in Southwark in the future lies in addressing perennial local issues – housing remains a priority today, as it was fifty years ago – as much as in reinventing the borough. The projects illustrated in this book represent more than two decades of rediscovery and renewal, a process set to continue with renewed energy during Southwark's third millennium.

During the 1950s and 1960s much of Southwark was redeveloped with local authority housing, often in the form of towers or slabs. Shown above and opposite is the Elmington Estate in Camberwell.

Archaeology in Southwark
Sarah Gibson

One of the consequences of regeneration, particularly in the north of Southwark, is that it provides archaeologists with opportunities to carry out excavations before construction of new developments. Since 1990 archaeology has been considered during the planning process, and, although sometimes not welcomed by developers, recent discoveries have greatly increased our knowledge. The pieces of this archaeological jigsaw fit together over time, but the overall picture of Southwark's rich past has yet to be fully revealed.

Human occupation of the borough commenced at least 10,000 years ago with groups of Mesolithic hunter-gatherers exploiting the wetlands and islands of the southern Thames shore. The Old Kent Road, now thronged with superstores, operated as a major flint-implement manufacturing site, where nearly 2000 carefully chiselled tools, such as arrow heads, have been found. In the north of the borough, prehistoric farmers left the marks of their primitive ploughs fossilized on island surfaces, once surrounded by marsh and water, and now buried beneath busy streets. One of those ancient islands was found at the site of CZWG's Bankside Lofts (see pp. 74–75), where archaeologists also discovered the remains of Bronze Age hut-circles.

There has been continuous settlement around the southern bridgehead of London Bridge since the Romans built the first bridge over the Thames shortly after their occupation in AD 43. The Roman settlement, once thought to have been a minor suburb of the great city on the north bank of the Thames, has acquired a new significance, discovered in part by the excavations for the Jubilee Line Extension (see page 61). Beneath Borough High Street, Roman buildings, of simple clay and timber construction, were occupied by bakers and blacksmiths and stood adjacent to a market hall with a colonnade. The settlement was approximately 24 ha (60 acres) in size, with major roads leading to and from it. Adjacent to the roads,

the Romans buried their dead. In 2001 the biggest Roman cemetery in Southwark was found on America Street, where 168 burials were discovered, many with grave goods. More evidence of the Roman settlement, in the form of domestic buildings and roads, has been found at excavations preceding development at Borough Market and Southwark Cathedral (see pp. 84–87). At the latter, a stretch of Roman road is left on permanent display beside the remains of the cloister of the medieval priory of St Mary Overie and a seventeenth-century delftware pottery kiln.

In 2002 a major religious establishment was uncovered at the south-east of this settlement. Two Romano-Celtic temples were found during excavations on Long Lane, set within a precinct lined with statues and adjacent to a villa where pilgrims may have stayed. A dedicatory inscription, probably from one of the temples, was set up to Mars Camulos by Tiberius Celerianus, a trader originating from Reims in France. The inscription refers by name to the Londinensi ('the people of London'), and is one of only two inscriptions yet discovered in Britain that refer directly to Londinium in any form.

The medieval settlements of Southwark hosted many influential institutions, notably the abbeys at Bermondsey and St Mary Overie. The twelfth-century Cluniac priory and abbey in Bermondsey was at the hub of the village until the Dissolution in the sixteenth-century. Set within a massive precinct part-surrounded by a wall, the abbey was accessed through the great gatehouse located at the junction of present-day Abbey Street and Bermondsey Street. Beneath the proposed development at Bermondsey Square Antiques Market (see pp. 122–23), the remains of the abbey's inner court and cloister lie hidden. As this is a scheduled ancient monument, the foundations of the new-build are being designed to preserve these historically significant remains for perpetuity, while still allowing for the regeneration of this

important urban space, left vacant since the end of the Second World War.

Other important residences of kings and nobility, such as the Great Hall of Winchester Palace and Edward III's moated manor house in Rotherhithe, still stand as stark contrasts to the Victorian warehouses and modern buildings constructed around them. Yet others survive only as archaeological monuments, however. On the Thames waterfront, Edward II built 'The Rosary', his summer palace, on what is now the site of the More London development (see pp. 94–95). The area also boasted tidal mills and Sir John Fastolff's moated manor house. Remnants of these grand houses and mills were recorded by archaeologists before development, and their story is told in an interactive display in the foyer of City Hall.

Bankside was part of the Bishop of Winchester's estate, despite the bawdy and uncontrolled activities that took place there. Within this area lie the remains of at least three Elizabethan and Stuart playhouses, and as many as four animal-baiting arenas. The location of the Rose and the Globe are known, but the site of the Hope, which served as a playhouse and a bear garden, remains a mystery. In 2001 the north-eastern quarter of a polygonal structure, which may be the Hope, was found beneath a demolished 1950s building fronting on to Bankside. It now lies beneath the new building, preserved for the future.

For regeneration to be truly successful, it has to create a sense of place and to integrate into the historical context treasured by a community. The popularity of the council's archaeology and outreach projects for participants of all ages illustrates how important the communities in Southwark consider their history to be. Archaeological excavation in advance of the projects described in this book has not only contributed to our knowledge of this most historic borough but added value to its regeneration.

Scenes and artefacts from archaeological excavations in Southwark: the wooden tip from a Bronze Age ard (plough) used by early farmers in Southwark (opposite); the stone floor from an eighteenth-century industrial building on Bankside (above left); the rose window in the Great Hall of Winchester Palace (above right); the inscription containing the reference to London, found at a site on Long Lane (top right); the remains of a Roman stone building at Borough Market (bottom left); and the possible remains of the Hope Theatre on Bankside (bottom right).

Projects

New Concordia Wharf
Mill Street, SE1

Pollard Thomas Edwards architects
1981–84

New Concordia Wharf was one of the pioneering projects on which the regeneration of Southwark's former docklands was founded. It provided a model for numerous subsequent residential conversions of former warehouses and factories across Britain.

The developer, Jacob's Island Company, led by Andrew Wadsworth, from Manchester, had the vision that large property companies lacked. The conventional approach to riverside development, involving demolition of most of the existing buildings, was represented by projects such as London Bridge City or, worse still, the King's Reach scheme near Blackfriars Bridge. Jacob's Island acquired the former flour mill adjacent to St Saviour's Dock in 1980 and appointed Nicholas Lacey as architect for the conversion scheme. Lacey, whose proposals for a radical make-over of the mill were unacceptable to his client, was later replaced by Pollard Thomas Edwards architects, and planning permission was granted by Southwark Council in 1981. In 1982 the late Victorian buildings were listed Grade II, so that listed-building consent for the conversion had to be secured.

Wadsworth's aim was, in fact, to retain the external appearance of the buildings virtually unchanged. The brickwork was cleaned and repaired. Missing original windows were replaced with exact replicas. The landmark chimney, the subject of a Dangerous Structures Notice, was retained and repaired. The principal change was the addition of balconies, in an appropriately nautical style, to the creekside façade. Internally, too, the stress was on preserving the character of the historic fabric as found. Working closely with engineers Alan Baxter & Partners, the architects devised innovative ways of fireproofing the brick, iron and timber structure so that original features could remain exposed – in the process, a thin layer of concrete was laid on top of the timber floors. The sixty apartments were sold as shells, to be fitted out by the buyers (prices ranged from £24,000 to £250,000) – a novel idea that quickly caught on. Wadsworth commissioned Piers Gough to fit out the former water tower of the complex as his own apartment, the first of a number of Docklands projects by Gough's practice, CZWG. Pollard Thomas Edwards architects subsequently worked with Jacob's Island on the masterplan for the Courage Brewery site and refurbished the former Anchor Brewhouse next to Tower Bridge, a project completed in 1989.

New Concordia Wharf was a pioneering reuse of industrial buildings unprecedented at the time. The scheme was launched by a young and inexperienced developer, Andrew Wadsworth, who had a clear vision of what could be achieved.

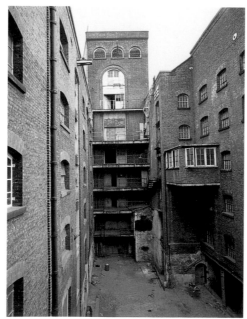

Thames Tunnel Mills
Rotherhithe Street, SE16
HTA Architects
1981–84

While Andrew Wadsworth was selling his version of loft living to affluent professionals at New Concordia Wharf, further to the east HTA Architects (then known as Hunt Thompson Associates) and its client, the London & Quadrant Housing Trust, were giving 'social' housing a new image at Thames Tunnel Mills.

The disued flour mill, close to Rotherhithe Church, originally of the 1850s but extended thirty years later, had been identified as a candidate for residential conversion by this conservation-minded architecture practice back in the late 1960s. However, it took many years before a client could be found who was willing to undertake what was in those days considered a radical scheme. Meanwhile, the buildings had suffered the ravages of fire and vandalism. Given their condition, and the tight budget for the project, complete internal reconstruction was the only course, and the original timber floors were replaced with reinforced concrete. Original beams and columns were salvaged, however, and reused in the seven-storey, toplit atrium that forms the new heart of the complex. This device solved the principal problem that the conversion project faced – securing adequate daylight in a very deep building. Elsewhere, a void that had housed a grain silo was used to contain a new lift and stairs. Externally, the brickwork was cleaned and repointed, and original windows repaired or replicated.

Thames Tunnel Mills was designed for young single people (71 flats, with accommodation for 119 occupants) and finishes were tough and basic. Communal facilities include a rooftop garden with terrific views of the river.

The conversion of Thames Tunnel Mills rescued a significant industrial complex from dereliction, while providing affordable housing for young people. By glazing over the central yard (above), the project created a social focus for the building.

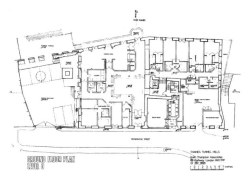

Hay's Galleria
Tooley Street, SE1

Michael Twigg Brown & Partners
1982–86

It is hard to imagine sailing ships berthed in what is now Hay's Galleria, but they were accommodated here in the nineteenth century, mostly for unloading foodstuffs. More recently, goods were transferred ashore here by lighter (a type of barge) – but the entire Hay's Wharf complex, which had suffered considerable war damage, closed during the 1970s and was partly demolished to make way for the London Bridge City development.

Hay's Dock itself, enclosed by warehouses of the 1860s, was retained, with the warehouses radically converted to offices and apartments, the dock covered by a pavement (removable, in theory, should anyone want to refill the dock in the future), and a steel-and-glass roof thrown over the entire space. At ground-floor level the galleria houses shops, bars and restaurants, and to make up for the lack of ships there is a 'kinetic sculpture' called *The Navigators*. The drained dock itself is now used as a car park.

The Civic Trust gave the galleria an award in 1989 – rightly so since, at the time, public space was at a premium in new Docklands developments. In fact, Hay's Galleria is private territory, gated after hours. Yet it is a popular place and continues to work well. It is interesting to imagine what Norman Foster or Richard Rogers might have done with it – certainly not a repro-Victorian roof structure. The Richard Rogers Partnership's unbuilt Coin Street scheme, designed for a site just upriver in Lambeth, would have featured a galleria of even grander dimensions, 800 m (half a mile) long.

Although the detail of its new roof is a pastiche of Victorian engineering, Hay's Galleria provides a valuable covered public space close to the river.

China Wharf
Mill Street, SE1

CZWG Architects
1982–88

An extraordinary sight still, and a striking contrast to the well-mannered conversion of the adjacent New Concordia Wharf, China Wharf was, in fact, built for the same client – the young developer Andrew Wadsworth – and the two projects' programmes overlapped. China Wharf was a landmark, equally, in the rise of CZWG: its first substantial new building and, the water tower apartment conversion at New Concordia Wharf aside, the first of a number of projects in Docklands and its hinterland, from Borough Market to the Isle of Dogs.

The colourful river façade of China Wharf is, in Piers Gough's own words, "part boat, part pagoda and very red". The building draws inspiration from traditional dockland silos and remains a landmark on this stretch of the Thames.

China Wharf replaced Reed's 'A' Wharf, an old warehouse abutting New Concordia Wharf, which, on account of its deep plan, had little potential for conversion. By the early 1980s, with the London Docklands Development Corporation in operation, a more permissive planning regime was in charge and the hope that former docks buildings would somehow revert to their earlier use was finally buried. The China Wharf scheme provoked a negative response from the then Royal Fine Art Commission, but won consent nonetheless. CZWG's Mill Street façade is well-mannered Repro-Warehouse. The southern façade takes its cue from dockland silos, its scalloped concrete form cleverly allowing for windows that look out of the rear access yard towards the rising sun. The river frontage consists of two elements: all-over glazing and a superimposed solid centrepiece of concrete, painted a bright red, with great arched openings. The concrete and the steel balconies are all painted – the architects, flouting Modernist orthodoxy, felt no obligation to distinguish between structural and non-structural elements. Inside, the flats are arranged on a scissor section, with access at alternate levels and all living spaces facing the river, with bedrooms to the rear. Piers Gough comments that the building is "part boat, part pagoda and very red, it is definitely waving, not drowning".

After China Wharf, Wadsworth and Gough planned their most spectacular collaboration to date, at Jacob's Island, a little further east. A mix of residential and commercial space, the scheme developed the idea of the 'Brighton effect' – the land would be artificially raised (with parking below) to create sloping streets, with views down to the Thames. On the relatively narrow river frontage, a 'sunburst' block would develop the theme of China Wharf on a larger scale. A series of towers rose beyond, addressing a central square. The range of materials was to include brick, glass, concrete and "a huge tidal wave of green copper". This scheme, which fell victim to the early 1990s recession, remains one of the great London 'unbuilts' of recent times. A far more pedestrian scheme, by Berkeley Homes, was subsequently built on the site.

Imperial War Museum Development
Lambeth Road, SE1

Arup Associates/DEGW
1983–2000

The formal opening on 6 June 2000, by Queen Elizabeth II, of the Imperial War Museum's Holocaust Galleries (designed by Stephen Greenberg of DEGW) also marked the completion of a three-stage development of the museum by Arup Associates, which had begun work on the project seventeen years before.

The Imperial War Museum is one of London's best museums, notable for its intelligent presentation of the issues surrounding human conflict and constituting far more than a collection of military hardware. (The museum has plenty of the latter, but also the best collection of twentieth-century British art outside the Tate.) The museum moved into the former premises of the Bethlehem Hospital ('Bedlam'), set in Geraldine Mary Harmsworth Park, in the 1930s. The long residential wings of the Regency building were demolished and the remaining accommodation was adapted to house displays of weapons and military history.

A matter-of-fact extension was built in the 1960s to house storage, offices and workshops. The commission to Arup Associates (in 1983) to develop a masterplan for the future of the museum reflected changing perceptions about its role: better visitor facilities, including provision for school parties, were needed as well as greatly expanded gallery spaces – a large proportion of the collection was then in storage. Expansion into the surrounding parkland was ruled out, so the museum had to intensify the use of its existing complex of buildings. The presence of the Bakerloo Underground line below the building placed severe constraints on subterranean development.

Phase I of the Arup project, constructed from 1988 to 1989 with the museum closed, was transformational in effect, giving the museum a dramatic new focus in the form of the great central atrium. The barrel-vaulted, toplit space provided an ideal place to show tanks, rockets and other large exhibits, and a cinema and two new gallery spaces were included in this phase of works. The remainder of the project was carried forward with the museum open to the public. Phase II, built from 1993 to 1994, created another 1600 sq m (17,000 sq ft) of gallery and exhibition space in the south-eastern lightwell of the building. Finally, from 1997 to 2000, a further 5700 sq m (61,000 sq ft) of galleries – largely the Holocaust Galleries – and education and conference spaces were added along the south-west side of the museum, and the lattice vault of the central atrium extended 40 m (130 ft) southwards over the new addition, covering an extended staircase and glazed lifts. The Holocaust Galleries were constructed on top of the existing cinema. Externally, the south-western extension is faced in stock brick to match that of the existing listed building – a seamless and unselfconscious continuation of the language of the original.

Externally discreet, Arup Associates' Imperial War Museum project has transformed the former hospital building internally to create a lofty toplit display and circulation space.

Butler's Wharf
Butler's Wharf, SE1

Conran Roche and others
1984—

Forty years ago, Butler's Wharf was quintessential Docklands. The critic Ian Nairn, writing in 1966, considered it "the grandest part remaining of the docks … You are not so much looking at part of London as walking about in it." In 1972 the wharf closed and its massive 1870s warehouses, extending across Shad Thames back to Gainsford Street (hence the dramatic bridges), stood empty for more than a decade – making it a natural habitat for film-makers in search of a slice of 'real' London. It could all have gone the way of the London Docks, demolished during the 1970s, but survived to be acquired – for £5 million – by a consortium that included Sir Terence Conran. By this time seventeen buildings at Butler's Wharf had been listed.

The aim was to convert the historic ware-houses to new apartments in the mould of New Concordia Wharf (see pp. 30–31). A masterplan for the 4.5 ha (11 acre) site was drawn up by Conran Roche, the architectural practice established by Terence Conran and Fred Roche in 1981, which moved its own offices to a converted building in the area. The practice was responsible for the new Design Museum (see pp. 44–45), opened in 1989. With Stuart Mosscrop as design supremo, Conran Roche was also responsible for a number of other buildings in the vicinity, including Cinnamon Wharf, a functional seven-storey warehouse recast as flats (completed in 1987); a student residence for the London School of Economics on Gainsford

Street (1989); Coriander Building, Gainsford Street (a conversion of warehouses into offices); and Saffron Wharf, a coolly Miesian office building overlooking St Saviour's Dock (1990). The conversion of the riverside warehouses into eighty-six apartments was completed in 1990 – a new concrete structure underpins the Victorian façades. The construction of Spice Quay, a new 18,000 sq m (190,000 sq ft) office building adjoining them to the east, was planned during the same year. Spanning Shad Thames, with shops and restaurants at street level, the steel-framed, heavily glazed building would have been Conran Roche's *chef d'œuvre* but fell victim to the early 1990s recession. An inferior building by another hand now occupies the site.

The Butler's Wharf project involved a radical remodelling of redundant nineteenth-century warehouses for shops, restaurants and apartments.

Horselydown Square
SE1

Wickham Van Eyck Architects
1985–91

Close to Tower Bridge and facing the Anchor Brewhouse on Shad Thames, Horselydown Square – like other pioneering developments in Docklands – was a collaboration between a new-generation architectural practice and an inspirational developer, in this instance the late Michael Baumgarten. Occupying most of the site of the former Courage Brewery, it forms one of the key elements in the regeneration of the riverside area bounded by Tower Bridge Road, Jamaica Road and St Saviour's Dock. Integrating new and revitalized old buildings, the mixed-use scheme – 4650 sq m (50,000 sq ft) of offices, seventy-six apartments plus retail and restaurant units – is, according to Julyan Wickham, "based on the premise that high density is both desirable and necessary to urban life … The programme is mundane: it includes no highlights and relies only on the fabric necessary to provide living and work spaces which make up the substance of the city."

The Buildings of England detected "affluent Continental … urbanity", while Stephanie Williams felt that "it goes somewhat overboard". Edward Cullinan, however, summed up the merits of the project, describing it as "an excellent bit of city". The key to its success lies first in its opening up of the traditionally closed city block, with two squares created between Shad Thames and Gainsford Street and connected by a narrow street (a memory of the old Docklands townscape) that provides a public route across the site. Secondly, the development is truly mixed use in a way that is more European than British, with buildings that contain shops and offices on lower floors and flats above. (Too often, funding institutions place an embargo on this eminently workable combination of uses.) Shops and restaurants at ground level bring the whole place to life. Finally, it is the excellence and appropriateness of the architecture – despite fudged detailing in places – that make

Horselydown Square an exemplar still for new urban architecture. Eclectic in inspiration, with clear references to classic Modern Movement sources – a memory of Bicknell & Hamilton's 1960s Paddington maintenance depot may be detected – the new buildings are rich in texture and colour, and strong and complex in form, with projecting balconies and glazed pavilions providing viewing points from many flats. The need to maximize daylight and views throughout the site was, of course, a key generator of the form of the buildings. Nearly twenty years after its conception, this project still commands respect, demands study and puts to shame many later developments that entirely lack its subtle understanding of urban decorum.

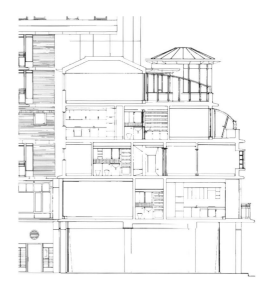

Colourful and shapely, the Horselydown Square scheme is particularly interesting for its creation of a new urban dimension to the area around Butler's Wharf, and for its opening up of a formerly enclosed city block long occupied by the Courage Brewery.

Conran Roche's revamp of a mundane 1950s warehouse gave London a forum for the display and presentation of modern design. It provided a striking contrast to the brick façades of the Butler's Wharf warehouses.

Design Museum
Shad Thames, SE1

Conran Roche/Stanton Williams
1987–89

The Design Museum was the creation of Sir Terence Conran, founder of the Habitat chain of stores and a key mover in the regeneration of Butler's Wharf (see pp. 40–41), and the design historian and commentator Stephen Bayley. Together they had established the highly successful Boilerhouse at the Victoria and Albert Museum, South Kensington, to raise public awareness of the importance of design, and the Design Museum was founded (and largely financed, via his charitable foundation) by Conran to develop this mission in a new setting.

The raw material was a utilitarian concrete-and-brick 1950s warehouse facing the river just east of Butler's Wharf. The building, which bridged the eastern end of Shad Thames, had one virtue, apart from its inherently solid construction: its stepped profile to the river. This was a fairly radical conversion – one entire floor was removed to create adequate head clearance, and a new floor constructed above the roof – though perhaps a little po-faced and too expressive of received 'good taste'. More rebuilding was done than was necessary, in fact, to avoid the imposition of Value Added Tax imposed on conversion projects (but not on new build) by the Thatcher government.

The end product is a building that pays homage to the 'White Modern' style of the 1930s while also recalling the more recent work of Richard Meier. Externally, it makes an attractive element in the riverside scene, framed by new staircase towers, and a neat contrast to the massive brick façades of the nineteenth-century warehouses and the colourful exuberance of Piers Gough's China Wharf (see pp. 36–37). Open terraces facing the river were created. The new metal-clad top floor is clearly expressed as an intervention. The gallery fit-out was entrusted to the safe hands of Stanton Williams, a practice then known chiefly for exhibition design, and resulted in interiors of real elegance. The most enjoyable part of the building is, however, the first-floor Blueprint Café, the first of Conran's eateries in the area and still perhaps the best.

The fit-out here reflects the personal input of Terence Conran, with something of the *joie de vivre* that pervaded the early Habitat stores. On a fine day, lunching at a table on the external terrace, with wonderful views of the river, is an experience to be relished.

The Circle
Queen Elizabeth Street, SE1
CZWG Architects
1987–89

The Circle is a test for taste. "An example of the architects' theatrical taste thrust on the public", wrote critic Stephen Gardiner, while *The Buildings of England* pronounces the scheme "one of the most extravagant pieces of architectural whimsy in London, rich enough to keep it from palling".

The Circle forms part of the remarkable area of new and reused buildings generated by the 1980s boom in the hinterland of Butler's Wharf, close to Tower Bridge. This is a lively, mixed-use urban quarter in which the promise of Docklands – recycling old buildings of value and, equally, producing new architecture of high quality – was, for once, convincingly realized.

The rationale behind the development was somewhat different from that at New Concordia Wharf or China Wharf (see pp. 30–31 and 36–37). The aim was to produce 'London pads' targeted at relatively young professionals, who might be weekly commuters. Fully equipped, in contrast to the unfitted shells offered at New Concordia Wharf, the flats had access to some of the facilities of a hotel – a gym and swimming pool, for example. Local shops were included in the scheme. The architecture first responds to the severe context of stock-brick warehouse canyons, then subverts the local vernacular to spectacular effect. At its core, the scheme moves from stock brick to brilliant blue-glazed brick for the 'circle' (the size of a gasometer) that is its central focus. Balconies are supported on concrete logs, a device also used in Piers Gough's house for journalist and broadcaster Janet Street-Porter in Clerkenwell. The entrance lobbies are, says Gough, "deliberately glam … this place was meant to be groovy, exciting – no hint of warehouse austerity here!" Gough's response to Stephen Gardiner was, incidentally: "He is right. But there is no point in being an architect without that confidence".

The Circle makes a very strong urban gesture, creating public space as well as private apartments. It remains one of the most striking residential developments in the riverside area.

Vogan's Mill
Mill Street, SE1

Squire & Partners
1987–89

Vogan's Mill, named after the family that ran a grain and cereal business on the site for over 170 years, was acquired in 1986 by developer Rosehaugh for conversion to residential use. Backing on to St Saviour's Dock – until the 1980s coasters unloaded grain directly into the mill – the complex consisted of nineteenth-century brick warehouses flanking some very inferior 1950s infill. The most prominent feature of the site, however, was a tall concrete silo. The existence of this local landmark provided a rationale for its replacement by a seventeen-storey apartment tower that was, at the time, the tallest new building in Docklands and is some 15 m (50 ft) higher than the silo, the existing concrete shell of which was retained as part of the development. The slender tower contains one apartment per floor, with a three-storey penthouse at the top.

With the 1950s additions demolished, a new apartment building was slipped in behind Mill Street – this is visible only from the dock. Most of the nineteenth-century fabric was carefully converted to flats, with the timber interiors and external fenestration retained intact. One block, however, fronting Mill Street, was in very poor condition and was demolished and rebuilt in replica. Courtyards were created to bring daylight into the depths of the site.

The style of Squire's new work, light and somewhat nautical in flavour, contrasts well with the solidity of nineteenth-century brickwork, and the result is a classic marriage of new and old.

The tower of Vogan's Mill was a pioneering tall building in this quarter of Docklands; however, the existing concrete silo on the site was retained and extended as part of Squire's residential conversion scheme. A new apartment building, visible only from the dock, was slipped in between existing warehouses.

David Mellor Building
Shad Thames, SE1

Hopkins Architects
1988–91

Master cutler and designer David Mellor has been the client for two of Michael Hopkins's best buildings: the factory at Hathersage, near Sheffield, completed in 1989; and the offices and showroom block close to Butler's Wharf. Although the building was later sold to Sir Terence Conran, it is appropriate that it bears the name of the enlightened client who commissioned it.

The six-storey building is conceived as a simple glazed box, with the top floor (where Mellor had an apartment) set back to provide roof terraces, and with service cores 'bookending' it to north and south in the best Kahnian 'served and servant spaces' tradition. The influence of Louis Kahn is evident, indeed, not only in the diagram of the building but equally in its aesthetics. The street elevation has strong echoes of Kahn's Mellon Center at New Haven, Connecticut.

Indeed, for Hopkins Architects (then known as Michael Hopkins & Partners), the project marked an important step forwards from a predominantly metallic architecture based on a 'kit of parts' philosophy towards a more obviously crafted approach. Like other architects of the 'High-tech' tradition, Hopkins had to get to grips with concrete. (Richard Rogers did so at Lloyd's of London.) The Mellor Building is concrete-framed, with the structure – round columns supporting flat slabs – externally expressed as a powerful frame for full-height glazing on the elevations to Shad Thames and St Saviour's Dock. The flank walls are clad in lead-covered panels. The ground floor formerly housed the Mellor shop, selling well-designed kitchen utensils.

The finish of the concrete was the subject of enormous effort by architect and client – Mellor reportedly hand-sanded the columns personally to secure the desired effect. For Hopkins's chronicler, Colin Davies, writing in 1993, "Hopkins's habitual truth to materials has never been more consistently expressed than at Shad Thames". That judgement arguably still rings true.

Exemplifying Hopkins's move from 'High-tech' into handcrafted architecture, the David Mellor Building remains one of the practice's finest works. Subsequently, it found a sympathetic new owner in Sir Terence Conran.

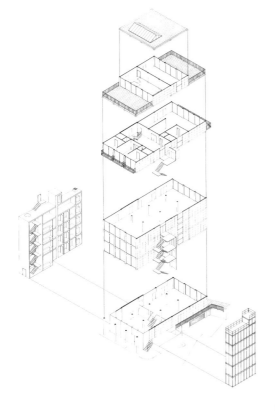

51

Globe Theatre
Bankside, SE1

Theo Crosby/Pentagram Design
1989—97

Director Sam Wanamaker conceived the idea of "creating a living, working monument to Shakespeare" on the banks of the Thames in 1949. The result, the new Globe Theatre, opened by Queen Elizabeth II in 1997 – both Wanamaker and his architect, Theo Crosby, had sadly died two years earlier – was the first thatched building erected in London since the Great Fire of 1666.

Tudor Bankside was, in the words of the historian A.L. Rowse, "a naughty neighbourhood" – famed for its brothels and its theatres, which thrived beyond the overbearing supervision of the city fathers. The original Globe, of which Shakespeare, actor–manager as well as playwright, was part-owner, was opened in 1599 using materials salvaged from a closed theatre in Shoreditch (also beyond the city boundaries). Reconstructed in 1614, with the thatched roof replaced by tiles, it was closed and demolished under the Commonwealth. Its location was some way to the south-east of the new Globe, across Southwark Bridge Road. The original site could not be reclaimed, but a more appealing one was found alongside the river, and a 125-year lease was secured from Southwark Council in 1982. Work on the foundations of the new Globe began in 1989, and work on the theatre and associated development for mixed use (including shops, apartments, a café and a small modern auditorium) started in earnest in 1992. The whole project was an extraordinary act of faith for all involved, especially Wanamaker, who had initially felt that "no one showed much interest in doing anything about a proper recognition of Shakespeare in the area of London where he lived and acted". The long gestation of the project reflects Wanamaker's struggle to raise the funding needed.

The designs for the new Globe (for an audience of 1500 – less than half the capacity of the original) were developed by Theo Crosby and his colleagues at Pentagram on the basis of historical and archaeological research. The decision was taken early on to create a timber-framed, thatched building, entirely traditional in construction. The theatre sits, however, on a great concrete raft, elevated above the river and clearly visible from the north bank. The basement areas contain a museum and other facilities. The new buildings around the theatre piazza are designed in a fanciful historicist manner that succeeds because of its sheer *jeu d'esprit* (by the 1980s Crosby had become disillusioned with Modernism). The Globe itself is a structure of green oak constructed by timber restoration specialist McCurdy & Co. The timber frame is infilled with lime plaster panels, which incorporate a fire resistant layer. Use of reed thatch for the roof also involved lengthy negotiations with fire officers – after all, the original Globe was destroyed by fire.

The Globe Theatre is, on one level, a magnificent folly and the fruit of one man's inspired obsession. But it provides a unique opportunity to see Shakespeare's plays performed as his contemporaries would have seen them, and a physical reminder that London, and Southwark in particular, was the breeding ground for his genius.

The new Globe Theatre was the first traditional timber-framed structure to be built in London since Raymond Erith's Jack Straw's Castle of the 1960s. Its reed thatched roof is certainly unique to this part of London.

Bermondsey Jubilee Line Station
Jamaica Road, SE16

Ian Ritchie Architects
1990–2000

Bermondsey Spa – which flourished briefly as a fashionable resort during the eighteenth century – has been long forgotten, but the water still bubbles up from the ground under high pressure around the site of Bermondsey station, providing a challenge to the design team for the station, which included civil engineer Sir William Halcrow & Partners and structural engineer Arup. A massive station box, contained within diaphragm walls engineered to withstand the pressure of the waterlogged soil, contains the platforms and public areas, and is braced by a series of open concrete trusses and flat slabs. The operational parts of the station are ingeniously threaded into this heroic structure, constructed on an island site bordered by the heavily trafficked Jamaica Road.

This section of the Jubilee Line Extension (JLE) was, in fact, made possible only by recent advances in tunnel-boring technology – it could not have been constructed in the days of Frank Pick and Charles Holden. Yet Bermondsey station is, in a sense, a latter-day successor to the 'neighbourhood stations' built on the extended Northern line by Holden in the 1920s. These new Underground stations of the inter-war years were the nodes for suburban growth, whereas Bermondsey is a marker for the regeneration of the inner city. Indeed, it is a testimony to the pioneering aspect of this project that the very need for a station in this somewhat bleak setting was established only after intense political lobbying.

Less obviously spectacular than the monumental stations at Canary Wharf and North Greenwich, Bermondsey nonetheless embodies as clearly as any on the line the principles of directness, legibility and clarity – with daylight filtered down to platform level – established by JLE chief architect, Roland Paoletti. Careful detailing, which includes platform benches designed by Ritchie (a rare departure from the standard platform fit-out on the JLE), provides a counterpoint to the nobility of the concrete structure. This is a model of what new transport buildings should be – and all the more significant for being located in a far from glamorous quarter of London.

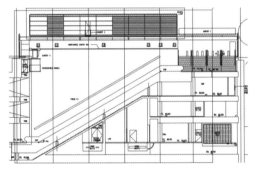

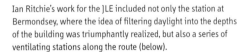

Ian Ritchie's work for the JLE included not only the station at Bermondsey, where the idea of filtering daylight into the depths of the building was triumphantly realized, but also a series of ventilating stations along the route (below).

Canada Water Jubilee Line Station and Bus Station
Surrey Quays Road, SE16

JLE Project Architects/Eva Jiricna Architects
1991–2000

In contrast to more accessible areas of Docklands, the former Surrey Docks, badly served by public transport, developed during the 1980s as an area of low-rise suburban housing punctuated by retail sheds and by printing plants serving newspapers that had relocated from Fleet Street. The only Underground connection was the East London line, itself poorly connected to the rest of the system, of which it formed a backwater.

The East London line passed through the site at Canada Water but there was no stop here – indeed, the site was part of the former Albion Dock. The new station, with attached bus station, is located where the East London and Jubilee lines cross diagonally, forming an important interchange. Canada Water was, in many respects, a pilot study for the other stations on the line – the first Jubiliee Line Extension (JLE) station to be designed, initially with Herron Associates as architects. The basic diagram is that of the Hong Kong Metro stations on which Roland Paoletti had worked before joining the JLE project. A box 22 m (70 ft) deep was dug by the cut-and-cover method. Toplit by a great lantern, recalling Charles Holden's Arnos Grove station of the 1930s and forming a beacon for the surrounding area, it contains three main levels: the concourse/booking hall, the East London line platforms and the Jubilee line platforms. The station's massive concrete structure provides a plinth for a future commercial development. Finishes are tough and functional – this was one of the most economical stations on the line, but it has a generosity of scale and rigorous functionality that are in tune with the great engineering traditions of the nineteenth century.

The adjacent bus station, providing connections to a wide area of south-east London, was designed by Eva Jiricna and has a light elegance that forms an admirable counterpoise to the 'muscle' of the Underground station. The overall glazed roof is sprung, via five slender steel columns, off a central spine that also contains passenger facilities. The main roof truss, 100 m (330 ft) long, is enclosed in toughened glass (ensuring that it is not a haven for pigeons). A swirling glass canopy connects the bus and Underground stations. Taken together, they form not only a much-needed transport connection but also a vital civic gesture in a somewhat featureless zone of Docklands.

Canada Water station is topped by a circular lantern filtering daylight down to the platform areas (left and opposite). Adjacent to the Underground station is a bus station with elegant canopies designed by Eva Jiricna (above).

Southwark Jubilee Line Station
The Cut/Blackfriars Road, SE1
MacCormac Jamieson Prichard
1991–2000

Most of the architectural practices selected by Roland Paoletti to work on the new Jubilee Line Extension (JLE) stations – Foster and Partners, Ian Ritchie, Wilkinson Eyre and Michael Hopkins, for example – come from a tradition of design, formerly called 'High-tech', in which the close interaction of architecture and engineering is taken for granted. Richard MacCormac is conspicuously not part of that tradition – the engineering element in his work is implied rather than strongly expressed. Yet at Southwark, MacCormac has created one of the most memorable of the JLE stations, which gives no impression that the architecture is merely a decorative trimming on the real 'works'.

The station, serving Tate Modern, the Globe and the Old Vic theatres as well as growing residential and working populations around The Cut, was always intended to connect to Waterloo East (formerly a bleak adjunct to the mainline station), and this dictated its location. At street level, despite its prominent corner site, the station has a modest presence: a commercial development, planned to sit on top of it, has yet to be built. The excitement lies below ground, where MacCormac provides travellers with what he describes as "an episodic journey" through a series of dramatic spaces. From the circular ticket hall, a few steps down from the street, escalators lead down to an intermediate concourse, 16 m (50 ft) high, toplit and featuring a great wall of curved blue glass designed in collaboration with artist Alexander Beleschenko. From here, more escalators, contained in tightly compressed shafts, descend to the Underground platforms via a barrel-vaulted lower concourse, while an access tunnel leads to the new Waterloo East ticket hall, wrapped around the elevated viaduct. This station is infrastructure, and art, of a high calibre.

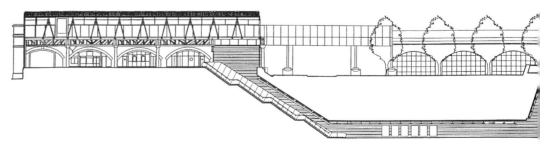

Richard MacCormac's Southwark Underground station features a series of dramatic spaces leading travellers via an intermediate concourse (above) to the barrel-vaulted lower concourse (opposite) and from there on to the platforms.

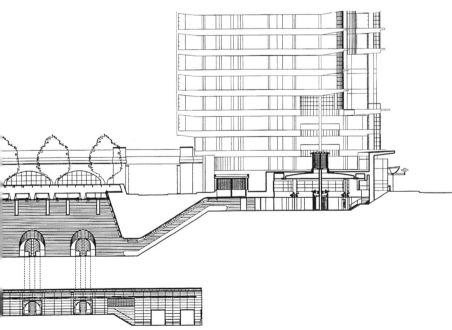

London Bridge Jubilee Line Station
Tooley Street/Joiner Street/Borough High Street, SE1
JLE Project Architects/Weston Williamson Architects
1990–2000

The Jubilee Line Extension (JLE) stations at Bermondsey, Canada Water and Southwark (see pp. 54–59) are entirely new creations, where no station existed until the advent of the extended line. At London Bridge the situation was radically different. The mainline station was the terminus of London's first railway line, opened in 1836 between here and Deptford – and soon extended to Greenwich. The Underground (in the form of the City & South London, later Northern, line), which had initially bypassed the station, arrived in 1900. There were tortuous connections between the Underground and the mainline platforms, which were raised above street level on a huge area of vaults and were awkwardly divided between through and terminating lines, and the general environment between them was hugely depressing.

The advent of the Jubilee line at London Bridge, with a fast connection to the West End via Waterloo, was a major gain for many users of the station and a clear boost for Bankside, fuelling the pressure for further commercial development in the area. The JLE project provided an opportunity to rebuild the Northern line platforms with much improved access, and equally benefited travellers using the main-line station. A new main concourse serving both lines was constructed off Tooley Street, abutting Joiner Street – a narrow and gloomy thoroughfare running below the mainline platforms. By closing Joiner Street, cleaning the brick vaults, paving and lighting the street and connecting it by escalators and lifts to the station above, a spacious and attractive new interchange has been created extending into former bonded stores. A second point of entry to the Underground was formed on Borough High Street, across the road from Borough Market, creating a gateway to the ancient heart of Southwark. It was here that archaeologists unearthed the remains of Roman shops, houses and a *macellum*, or market hall, with an open colonnade on to what later became Borough High Street. Some of the finds are displayed on site.

The technical problems in building the JLE through London Bridge were as complex as any encountered on the line, with services, sewers, piles and foundations forming a web of obstacles. The internal fit-out of the station was designed by Weston Williamson, with distinctive enamelled cast-iron panels used to line the platforms and escalator shafts.

Architects T.P. Bennett began work on a complete reconstruction scheme for the mainline station in 1998, with Wilkinson Eyre later brought in as collaborators. Topped by a 70,000 sq m (750,000 sq ft) office development, the new station was scheduled to open in 2007. At the time of writing, however, no definite timetable exists for the construction of this huge project.

At London Bridge the JLE project faced major engineering problems, but succeeded in making a convenient modern interchange out of one of the worst stations on the Underground system.

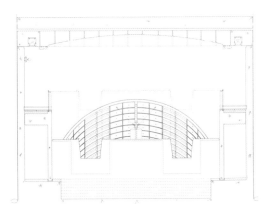

Camera Press Building
Butler's Wharf, SE1

Panter Hudspith Architects
1992–93

Located in the hinterland of fashionable Butler's Wharf, in an area where exuberant new buildings contrast with the monumental strength of (now refurbished) nineteenth-century warehouses, Panter Hudspith's Camera Press Building shows what can be made of an existing structure of distinctly modest interest.

The client was a photographic agency, and the brief was to provide offices and an exhibition gallery, to a tight budget, within the container of a converted 1960s warehouse block – the kind of building that might have been torn down without anybody much caring. In fact, this was a building with real strengths, notably the functional dignity of its concrete frame – left untouched externally and stripped of paintwork inside. Within the frame, new openings were formed and infilled with timber-framed glazing – full-height on the ground floor (where the gallery is housed), with solid panels on the upper floors made of untreated hardwood, which has already weathered to pleasing effect. Open corner balconies at first- and second-floor level provide a visual link with the architecture of CZWG's Circle (see pp. 46–47), just down the street. Side elevations are simply rendered. Much of the internal fit-out was constructed using timber recycled from the former loading-bay doors, which were a feature of the building's rear elevation. Everything is simple, dignified and economical: internal partition walls of exposed blockwork, services left equally unclad – reinforcing the strongly industrial, but far from uncomfortable, ethos of the internal spaces.

The most exciting space is located in an eyrie at the top of the building. Taking advantage of the height provided by a pitched roof, the architects introduced a steel-framed mezzanine level with workspaces – Camera Press's extensive archive is housed below.

The total cost of this project was under £350,000 – a fraction, of course, of that of a new building of comparable size. The project underlines the degree to which Southwark and other areas of London offer a resource (though one being steadily eroded by development) of low-cost buildings ideal for the needs of new and small businesses.

A low-cost recycling of a redundant warehouse, the Camera Press project is distinguished by its simple dignity and careful attention to the appropriate use of materials.

Peckham Pulse and Arch
Peckham High Street, SE15

Southwark Building and Design Service/Troughton McAslan
1993–98

Will Alsop's spectacular and now-famous Peckham Library (see pp. 88–89) is one element in a regeneration project intended to give Peckham a new social heart: breathing new life into an area where traditional retailing has taken a knock from the rise of the superstores but which retains its vitality nonetheless.

Troughton McAslan's arch forms a gateway to the new public square, an unashamedly symbolic gesture (although incorporating four shop units) that some critics felt was irrelevant to the needs of a far from affluent area. Clad in a waterproof membrane, the structure was, in fact, intended to provide shelter for market stalls and public entertainment, such as street theatre, and benefited from a lighting scheme by the artist Ron Haselden.

The £10 million Peckham Pulse, seen as a natural successor to the Pioneer Health Centre of the 1930s (with its emphasis on prevention rather than cure), was developed by Southwark Council – in collaboration with the local health authorities, and with backing from the Sports Lottery – as "a unique leisure, health and fitness resource that encourages and informs local people to invest in their own health and well-being". Opened in 1998, it contains swimming pools, gyms, exercise and dance studios, a crèche, and physiotherapy and consulting rooms – all the facilities (and more) that one would expect of an expensive private health club, and available to all. The aim was to create a building that was enjoyable and deliberately 'non-institutional'. The local authority team responded to this brief

with enthusiasm, producing a colourful and architecturally dynamic structure that refuses to be outfaced by Alsop's library. Internally, natural light is used to excellent effect and the emphasis is on transparency rather than enclosure – a moveable screen can be used to enclose the pool area when it is used for therapeutic treatment sessions, and a café looks out over the square.

The square itself was also designed by the local authority team under David Bradley and uses a variety of materials – tarmac, wood (recycled railway sleepers), and natural and artificial stone – to form a collage linking the new buildings. Artworks and a lighting scheme animating the surface of the square by night are further ingredients in this tough and practical, but also enjoyable, slice of urban landscape.

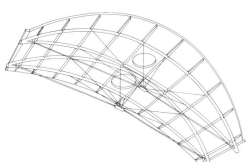

Alongside the Peckham Library, by Alsop Architects, the Peckham Pulse, a pioneering health and leisure centre, and Troughton McAslan's arch form the key features of a new square that provides a reinvigorated heart to Peckham.

Tate Modern
Bankside, SE1

Herzog & de Meuron
1994–2000

Tate Modern is a landmark not just in Southwark but also on the world cultural scene. It is no longer a novelty and the wave of excitement that accompanied its opening in 2000 has subsided, but Tate Modern's huge appeal to a wide public reflects the vision of Tate director Sir Nicholas Serota and his team. (It was Serota's then deputy, Francis Carnwath, who first recognized the potential of the redundant Bankside Power Station to house the Tate's modern collections, then in search of a new home.)

Following the decision to proceed with the acquisition of Bankside, a building completed as late as 1955, an international design competition was launched in 1994, with the Swiss practice of Herzog & de Meuron beating Tadao Ando, David Chipperfield, Rem Koolhaas, Rafael Moneo and Renzo Piano to win the commission. For admirers of Sir Giles Gilbert Scott's building, this was good news, since relatively minor changes were proposed to the external envelope – some contenders had suggested the demolition of the landmark chimney – while the monumental turbine hall inside was to be retained as a public forum.

Four years on, with many millions of visitors having passed through the building, the short-comings of the conversion are evident. Vertical circulation is not well handled. The galleries, and public facilities such as the restaurant, seem cramped and crowded in comparison with the huge volume of the Turbine Hall. And the crude 'collar' applied to Scott's chimney is an inelegant and apparently pointless addition.

Yet Tate Modern is a project still in development. Large areas of the building, including the part that still houses a big electrical substation, remain available for future conversion. And it would be hard to label the Turbine Hall 'wasted space' after stunning installations by Louise Bourgeois, Anish Kapoor, Olafur Eliason and others. As an engine of regeneration, Tate Modern has had a spectacular effect, confirming the rise of Bankside as a dynamic commercial and cultural quarter.

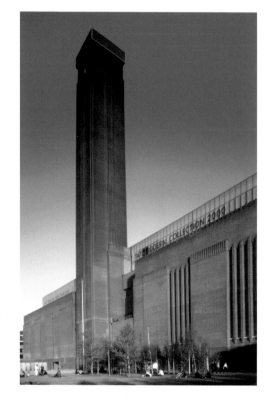

The plan (far right) shows the whole area of the building, including the areas on the south side yet to be colonized by the Tate. The vast Turbine Hall (above right) forms one of the most spectacular public spaces in Europe.

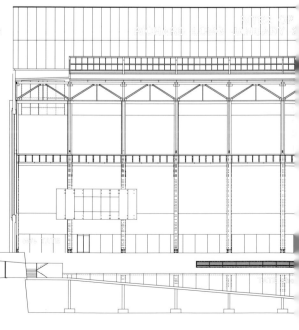

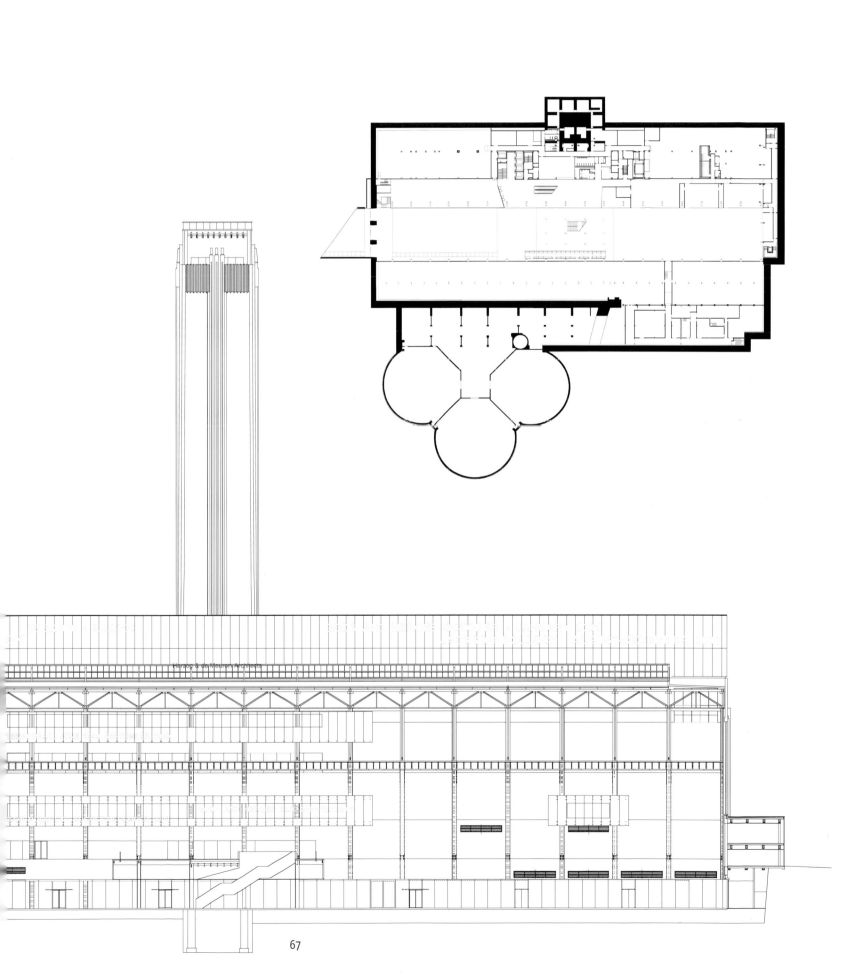

Herzog & de Meuron Architects

Oxo Tower Wharf
Barbe House Street, SE1
Lifschutz Davidson
1994–96

The Oxo Tower is a much-loved feature of the South Bank scene, part of a 1928–30 reconstruction of what had been a generating station for use as a meat store. Architect A.W. Moore arranged the windows in his tower to form the letters OXO, the name of a brand of stock cubes, so breaching a ban on advertisements along the river.

Lifschutz Davidson's client for the £20 million refurbishment of the entire building as flats, shops, workshops and restaurants was Coin Street Community Builders. The organization had inherited land along the river behind Stamford Street from the Greater London Council, following the abandonment of plans (including a visionary scheme by Richard Rogers) for large-scale commercial development there. Lifschutz Davidson also designed new social housing for the same client, just across the borough boundary in Lambeth.

The building was unlisted, which allowed the architects a free hand in realizing a brief that included the provision of affordable housing, workspaces for design industries, and retail and catering space. The industrial character of the building was respected in the conversion, which involved major repairs to the brickwork and the introduction of three new vertical cores for circulation and services. New steel-and-timber balconies animate the riverside façade.

One of the bolder ideas behind the scheme was the juxtaposition of affordable housing (seventy-eight flats for people working locally) with luxury dining. The existing roof has given way to a striking double-height glazed pavilion with a restaurant and bar run by Harvey Nichols. The views of the river and adjacent City, whether by day or night, are spectacular.

Lifschutz Davidson gave new life to this riverside landmark. The rooftop restaurant was designed by Julyan Wickham.

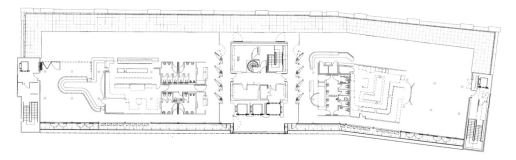

St Barnabas Church
Calton Avenue, SE21

HOK International
1995–96

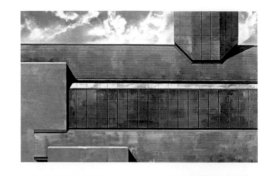

Churches, at least in Britain, do not form a significant proportion of the workload of HOK, a major international practice more accustomed to big commercial, public and masterplanning commissions. Indeed, new churches are a rare commodity in London. St Barnabas, Dulwich, was built after a ferocious fire destroyed the original church (a building of 1892–95 in the Perpendicular Gothic style by W.H. Wood) around Christmas 1992. A competition was organized in 1993 to select an architect for the new church, with HOK the clear winner. Construction of the new building began in 1995, and it opened in the autumn of 1996.

Following the destruction of the old St Barnabas, extensive discussions had taken place in the parish about the form and character of the new building. It was felt that the latter should, like its predecessor, be a landmark in the area, but that it should also respond to changing approaches to liturgy and to the need to provide

social as well as worship space – while offering a real sense of the sacred and numinous. There had to be the flexibility to adapt the interior for larger or smaller congregations (up to a maximum of 650 people) as the need arose. The requirement for a landmark was addressed by the building's crowning feature, the glass spire designed in collaboration with engineer Mark Whitby. The spire sits above the centralized sanctuary, enclosed by eight massive brick piers and containing the altar set below a striking corona. The font salvaged from the old church was set at the west end. Given St Barnabas's strong musical tradition and the desire to use the church for concerts as well as worship, acoustics were a major issue, and the slatted timber ceilings, formed as barrel vaults, were designed to provide an appropriate resonance. The predominant impression of the interior is one of subtly controlled but generous natural light – this is a building that opens up to its

surroundings as a Gothic Revival church never could. Another element that contributes to the success of the internal space is the range of furnishings designed by Luke Hughes – the stackable benches, rather than chairs, are a particularly happy addition. Using chairs, says Hughes, people cannot "squash up" on a big occasion, while conventional pews impose an inflexible arrangement. On big occasions at St Barnabas, the partitioned side chapel and meeting rooms can be opened up to the main space to provide extra seating. Comfortable and reassuring, rather than challenging, this building might seem typical of 'middle of the road' Anglicanism. But it manages to be both a community asset, with the element of outreach that its congregation sought, and a structure that has roots in tradition. The architects trod a difficult path that could have produced a fudge, but the end result is a memorable and popular piece of new architecture.

Internally, St Barnabas Church is an impressive daylit space, topped by a highly sculptural barrel vault formed of slatted timber. The exterior evokes the landmark quality of the former church on the site.

Dulwich Picture Gallery Extension and Restoration
College Road, SE21

Rick Mather Architects
1995–2000

As it is set in a suburban location, with rather poor public transport connections, one would assume that the Dulwich Picture Gallery might struggle to attract visitors. Yet its superb collection, excellent exhibitions and dynamic education programme have made it a destination for both tourists and south Londoners, while architects come from around the world to see one of the major works of that uniquely inventive classicist, Sir John Soane.

Soane was appointed in 1811 to design the gallery as a condition of the bequest to Dulwich College of the great collection of pictures formed by Noel and Margaret Desenfans and Sir Francis Bourgeois, a friend of the architect. A further, extraordinary, condition was that a mausoleum for the Desenfans and Bourgeois should be built as an adjunct to the gallery. Almshouses were also to be provided on the site; they were closed in the 1880s. Soane's building, completed in 1814, consisted of five galleries, with the mausoleum and almshouses forming a range to the west. It was never large enough for the collection. Soane wanted more gallery space and had drawn up plans for a cloister-like extension to the east. Even after the conversion of the almshouses to stores and offices, and the addition of a run of galleries along the eastern edge of the building (obscuring Soane's work), space remained tight. The Picture Gallery suffered severe war damage and a 1950s rebuilding was necessarily economical. By the 1990s it lacked the facilities (a café, lecture theatre and education space) that were by this time considered vital to any major museum – a headache for the trustees, who had taken over management of the gallery from the college.

Mather's competition-winning proposals won Lottery support following the failure of earlier funding attempts. The £6.5 million project has provided a café, an education studio and a multi-purpose lecture hall/display space (not to mention an adequate supply of WCs) located along a glazed cloister east of the gallery, and screened from the street by a brick wall – a rebuilding and extension of an existing wall. The Soane building has been comprehensively refurbished, with restoration of the original decorative scheme ('Picture Gallery red'), which had been researched by Ian Bristow in 1980; seamless installation of up-to-date environmental, lighting and security systems; and the creation of additional hanging space on the former almshouses site. Offices and stores have been decanted to the adjacent Old College buildings and redundant walls removed to open up views of the gallery from the south. The combination of understated, but elegant and well-detailed, additions and faithful restoration, using technologies not available to Soane, is irresistible.

Rick Mather's additions to the Dulwich Picture Gallery form a cloister connecting Soane's iconic building with the former college buildings (opposite) and providing much-needed visitor and educational facilities.

Bankside Lofts
Hopton Street, SE1

CZWG Architects
1996–98

CZWG's triumphant return to Southwark's riverside was designed for a client, Harry Handelsman of the Manhattan Loft Corporation, for whom the practice had already worked on a number of projects – beginning with a loft conversion at Summers Street, Clerkenwell. Handelsman had also been one of the developer team for the Circle (see pp. 46–47), close to Butler's Wharf. The project is a collage of old and new, seamlessly knitted together. At the core of the mixed-use office and residential development is a group of former industrial buildings, somewhat battered by wartime bombing, reused for their resource value rather than their historic or aesthetic interest. Attached is the new residential tower, rendered yellow, spiralling and stepping up from the south to provide all the apartments with fine river views – which are particularly splendid from the penthouse, one of the most desirable in London.

Retail space is provided at street level, while a first-floor piazza is screened by a massive timber fence. A new residential block contains the piazza to the east and the south. Bankside Lofts was a natural spin-off from the Tate's decision to locate its modern art gallery at Bankside, and, according to Piers Gough, won "effortless planning permission" from Southwark Council. A somewhat taller tower proposed for an adjacent site subsequently proved more controversial.

CZWG also designed Bankside Studios, a colourful office conversion of another group of industrial buildings on Southwark Street, for the Manhattan Loft Corporation.

The stepped tower of Bankside Lofts was designed to maximize views of the river from different apartments. Attached is a converted group of former industrial buildings, housing offices and retail space.

Odessa Wharf
Odessa Street, SE16

Torben Rix/Fletcher Priest Architects
1996—2000

Where building in tune with waterfront sites is concerned, Scandinavians – whose capital cities all front the sea – might seem to have a head start. It is not surprising then that Odessa Wharf, one of the most distinctive housing developments in the Docklands, was initiated by a Danish developer with Danish architect Torben Rix as consultant to Fletcher Priest. The development contains serviced accommodation, mostly rented to Scandinavians visiting London on business.

Odessa Wharf, on the further side of Surrey Docks, facing Canary Wharf, was once a point of entry to London for goods from the Ukraine. The surrounding area has been uninspiringly redeveloped since the closure of the Surrey Docks, but Fletcher Priest's project injects into it an element of quality, with a real feeling for place. The judges for the 1999 Housing Awards declared that it "shines out like a good deed in a generally naughty Thames-side-world".

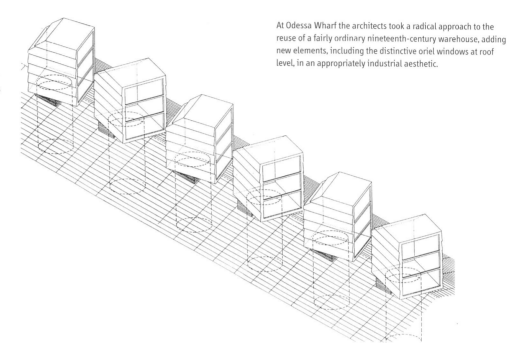

At Odessa Wharf the architects took a radical approach to the reuse of a fairly ordinary nineteenth-century warehouse, adding new elements, including the distinctive oriel windows at roof level, in an appropriately industrial aesthetic.

The raw material was an existing nineteenth-century warehouse, stout and handsome though not architecturally remarkable, standing at right angles to the Thames. The location explains the most distinctive feature of the conversion scheme, the series of glazed and timber-clad cowls along the roof. These not only admit light to top-floor rooms, but can also be accessed via spiral stairs for a view across the river. The two-storey building was divided to form eight apartments, 'bookending' a central run of six town houses. 'Bolt-on' metal-framed oriel windows provide oblique views of the river from all the units – and ensure that they are not overlooked by neighbouring properties. The original roof structure was retained, and provides a prominent feature of the internal spaces – though new floors and cross walls were inserted. The uncompromising industrial style of the new additions, and the high quality of detailing throughout, sets this scheme apart from the general run of Docklands conversions.

Millennium Bridge
Bankside, SE1

Foster and Partners/Arup
1996–2001

One of the most widely admired of London's millennium projects, the Millennium Bridge is a stunning marriage of architecture and engineering that reflects both architect and engineer on top form. The sculptor Sir Anthony Caro was also involved in developing the successful competition scheme of 1996, though his ideas for the landward terminations of the bridge were not realized.

The bridge opened in June 2000, when 100,000 people crossed it in the course of one weekend – and was promptly closed again after a pronounced 'wobble' developed. Technical adjustments – the fitting of dampers below the bridge deck – took over a year to complete, but the bridge, which is 320 m (1050 ft) long, is now a heavily used route between the City and Southwark, connecting the tourist magnets of St Paul's Cathedral and Tate Modern. This is the first Thames bridge designed specifically for pedestrians, and the first new crossing over the river since Waterloo Bridge.

The teething troubles of the project stem partly, perhaps, from its high ambitions. Foster and his multi-disciplinary team wanted to create a structure of extreme delicacy – a ribbon of steel by day, a blade of light by night – its minimalism capitalizing on the thrill of walking high above a great expanse of flowing water. In structural terms this is a suspension bridge, but the cables that support the deck – springing from two Y-shaped armatures sunk into the river bed – rise little more than 2 m (7 ft) above the deck, so that views from the bridge are maximized and its intrusion into the river scene minimized. It was a daring strategy, but it has paid off in terms of the visual impact of the structure. The bridge is anchored at each end by massive abutments, which necessitated deep excavations: this resulted in some interesting archaeological discoveries. At the City end the remains of waterfront wharves and buildings, dating from the twelfth century onwards, were of good-quality stone, while on the Southwark side the buildings had been of timber – a reflection of the lower status of the South Bank.

The "wobbly bridge", as some persist in describing it, is one of the incontestably great new sights of London and one of Norman Foster's most notable contributions to the reconstruction of the capital.

The Millennium Bridge has opened up a new pedestrian route across the Thames, and has accelerated the process of regeneration and development in Bankside.

Architects' Offices
Tanner Street, SE1

Weston Williamson Architects
1996–2001

Weston Williamson's decision to relocate its offices to Southwark was a direct result of the practice's work on the Jubilee line station at London Bridge. "We had got to know the area around London Bridge", partner Chris Williamson recalled. "We had many meetings with the planners and were impressed – Southwark is genuinely interested in modern design."

Although Weston Williamson had looked at the possibility of converting an old building, the partnership was attracted to the idea of creating something new that would contribute to the local context – a matter of "putting your money where your mouth is", according to Williamson. The opportunity arose with the commission to work on a housing development for the former Sarson's Vinegar Works, off Tower Bridge Road. The new four-storey office block forms part of a mixed-use scheme, along with thirty apartments, and Weston Williamson acted as project manager for the office element, employing its own subcontractors.

The office building on Tanner Street is an elegantly detailed exercise, in the Miesian manner: clean-cut and highly transparent, and with a low-energy services strategy. The intention is to landscape the small square that faces the street, and perhaps to open a café there for public use.

Economical but elegant, Weston Williamson's office on a former industrial site is one of the best smaller new buildings enlivening this area of Southwark.

Jerwood Space
Union Street, SE1

Paxton Locher Architects (Phase 1)/
Satellite Design Workshop (Phase 2)
1997–98

The chief aim of the Jerwood Space is to foster new talent and to support young artists by providing a cluster of high-quality rehearsal studios for theatre and dance. Its success lies in its informality and flexibility. In addition to the rehearsal studios, there is an impressive gallery space, a café and studio-offices for use by architects, photographers and dance and music companies, the income from which underpins the core activity of providing good, affordable space. The project takes no public money, and the Lottery grant for the initial refurbishment, which cost £1.4 million, was repaid by the Jerwood Foundation.

Jerwood Space was originally a plain but serviceable Victorian school building that needed a new use. Paxton Locher's approach was to conserve as much as possible of what existed, with even the cast-iron radiators reused – the architects' approach was described by *The Architects' Journal* as a matter of "inspired pragmatism". The existing wall and floor finishes

were cleaned up and retained – after 100 years of wear, they will probably last another century. Studio spaces and offices are accommodated in the main school block; a new lift tower provides disabled access to the upper level. The gallery and café are housed in former outbuildings, connecting the school to the street. A glazed wall opens on to an external events and dining area, now referred to as the 'Glasshouse' following the addition in 2003 of a glazed roof and three further glazed walls by Satellite Design Workshop. Otherwise, the existing structure has been retained and refurbished, with the lofty steel truss roof providing a generous display space, lit by existing north-facing roof lights. The management of natural light has been one of Paxton Locher's strengths, reflected in all its projects.

The success of the space is clear from the buzz of activity there. It is a precious resource for the London arts scene, but also an object lesson in putting ordinary buildings to good use.

Jerwood Space, a mix of refurbishment and new-build by Paxton Locher and Satellite Design Workshop, provides a highly flexible venue for young artists in the heart of Southwark.

Southwark Cathedral Millennium Project
London Bridge, SE1

Richard Griffiths Architects
1997–2001

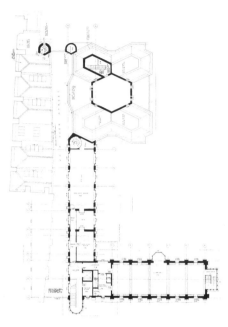

The new buildings at Southwark Cathedral seek to re-create something of the layout of the long-lost medieval monastic buildings to provide modern visitor facilities for the cathedral.

Southwark is one of England's smallest cathedrals – indeed, the church of St Mary Overie, originally attached to an Augustinian monastery, became the seat of a bishop only in 1905. (For many centuries, London south of the river was part of the diocese of Winchester, hence the presence close to London Bridge of Winchester Palace.) Yet the Anglican cathedral – Roman Catholics have their own cathedral a mile or so away – is not only a potent reminder of Southwark's long history, but also a medieval building of remarkable quality, though the nave is a confident late Victorian replacement for the original scandalously demolished in 1838.

Surrounded by warehouses, markets and railway tracks, and latterly by offices and flats, the cathedral lacked the cloisters and lawned close traditionally associated with its medieval counterparts. All its monastic buildings had long vanished. The regeneration of the Bankside area, in particular the Tate Modern project (see pp. 66–67), drove the cathedral authorities to reconsider the role of the building as a spiritual and community resource – and the destination for a steadily increasing flow of visitors. A chapter house and offices (by architect Ronald Sims) had been built north of the nave and adjacent to the vestries in 1987–88, and were integrated into the development project designed by cathedral architect Richard Griffiths (with Ptolemy Dean as project architect) and part-funded by the Millennium Lottery. The brief was to provide a new library, refectory, shop and meeting rooms – all fully accessible and addressing the pedestrian route along the river, from which the cathedral was isolated beyond a car park.

The acquisition of a Victorian building close to the east end of the cathedral provided a place to decant administrative functions, and also opened up a pedestrian route along the north side of the building. The new refectory and library block is located at right angles to cathedral. A glazed cloister or 'street' connects it with the chapter house (now used as an exhibition space) and vestries. The former car park has given way to a garden on the site of the medieval cloisters, part of a sensitive landscape scheme for the entire precinct by Elizabeth Banks Associates. The cathedral itself was cleaned and relit as part of the project, which also generated important archaeological investigations and the commissioning of several outstanding artworks.

The architecture of the new additions defies easy categorization. Using modern structural means (steel-framed glazing in the cloister, precast concrete for the library and refectory block) alongside traditional craftsmanship in stone, timber and metalwork – and inflecting everything with a pronounced Arts and Crafts voice – Griffiths has created something unique in London. The library – with precast concrete ribs, Gothic in form, supporting a fine timber roof – is a splendid example of rational building that would surely command the respect of the medieval craftsmen who created the cathedral.

Borough Market Regeneration
Off Borough High Street, SE1
Greig & Stephenson
1997–2004

Borough Market is a legendary London institution. In contrast to Covent Garden, now a specialist shopping centre appealing mainly to tourists, Southwark's Borough Market remains a real market, a place where Londoners go "foraging for fresh food", according to *The Observer*.

The present status of Borough Market, in fact, extends back considerably less than a decade. For many centuries – its origins lie in Norman times – the market operated from Borough High Street until it was removed (as a traffic obstruction) to its present site in the mid-eighteenth century. The character of the market as it now exists is indelibly stamped by the railway viaducts that cut dramatically through it, carrying trains into Cannon Street and Charing Cross stations, and closely abutted by market buildings ranging in date from 1850 to 1930. Until very recently, the market was exclusively wholesale; now it serves both the trade and, two days a week, the public. This is the only London wholesale market still operating largely on its original site.

The threat to the market from the Thameslink project – which demands a new rail viaduct across the site, necessitating the demolition of some early twentieth-century sheds – coincided, ironically, with the development of its expanded role. But the future of Borough

Market, now owned by an independent charitable trust, seems assured. Greig & Stephenson's major development project began in 1997 and continues. The market buildings are being progressively refurbished for their existing or – in some cases – new uses. (A shed on Cathedral Street has become the Fish! restaurant, with interior fit-out by Julyan Wickham.) Services and infrastructure are being upgraded, and clearer routes for the public created. When the Thameslink project is implemented – and the schedule for it remains unclear – the market will recolonize the spaces under and around it.

Historic buildings tend to remain rooted to their sites, but Borough Market has gained one that badly needed a home. The 1859 portico of the Floral Hall, dismantled to make way for the Royal Opera House development at Covent Garden and stored in pieces for years, has been reassembled on Stoney Street, where it replaces a nondescript 1950s shed. The elaborate silver iron-and-glass structure is a surprising presence in the narrow side street. Inside, it houses an elegant restaurant at first-floor level, and a new extension has been designed in an unashamedly contemporary manner. The Borough used to be known as "London's Larder" – it is good to see a great tradition reborn.

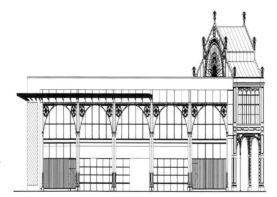

As part of the regeneration of Borough Market, part of the former Floral Hall from Covent Garden has been restored and reassembled to form the frontispiece to a striking new building.

Peckham Library
Peckham Square, SE15

Alsop Architects
1998–2000

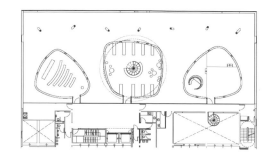

Will Alsop's Peckham Library, winner of the Stirling Prize in 2000, remains one of the most talked-about recent buildings in Britain. In a more 'sensitive' location and in a more conservative borough, Alsop's project might never have been built, yet it has been a shot in the arm for one of the less affluent areas of Southwark and has proved a popular success with the local community.

Part of a group of public buildings around the new Peckham Square (see pp. 64–65), intended to give the centre of Peckham the 'heart' it previously lacked, the library was commissioned by Southwark Council, which organized a series of competitive interviews in 1995. The brief was radical: to redefine the idea of a public library, reaching out to those who might never have been inside one before. The needs of young people and ethnic minorities were a particular concern, and while there would be no lack of books, access to new information technology would also be freely offered. This was to be a building for the local community, attractive but not prescriptive, serious but also enjoyable. Alsop defined it as "a meeting place, a debating place, a learning place, a peaceful place amidst the noise of the centre of town".

The library is elevated 12 m (40 ft) above Peckham Square, so that there are views out to the City and West End, only a few miles distant. Clad in patinated copper, with a bold red 'tongue' protruding at roof level, it is set on top of a vertical block – glazed with a mix of clear and coloured panels, and containing offices and staff facilities – and cantilevered across the square on a series of slender steel columns. The overhang provides a sheltered space that encourages the curious to venture inside. The main reading room houses three timber 'pods', built like boats, containing a meeting room, children's library and Afro-Caribbean library, and set apart from the activity below. Seats in the library are frequently at a premium.

This is a tough and practical building, designed for intensive use and hard wear. It has colour and style but is essentially streetwise, reflecting the character of Peckham, to which it responds with warmth and without condescension. Alsop is a passionate advocate of community architecture: "this building is there to be enjoyed", he insists. It appears that this is one building that is very much enjoyed, and loved, by its users. It has put Peckham on the architectural map of Europe.

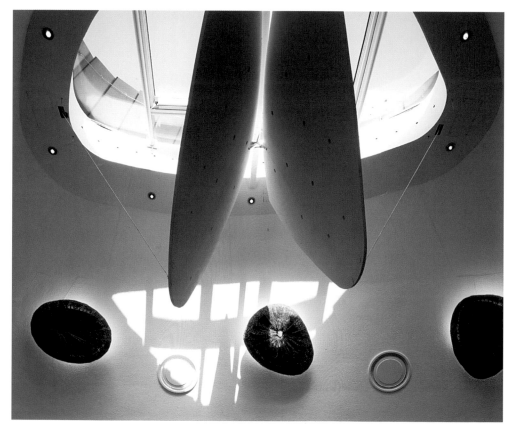

Peckham Library forms the focus of the new Peckham Square, a
local landmark. It represents the rethinking of the library as a
community resource as much as a repository of information.
Timber 'pods' house specific functions (opposite) for the meeting
room, children's library and Afro-Caribbean library.

House, Studios and Flats
King's Grove, SE15

Quay 2C Architecture
1998–2002

Regeneration projects come in all shapes and sizes. The conversion and extension of this former milk depot in Peckham into a private house, design studios and flats may lack the scale of Tate Modern (see pp. 66–67) or the glamour of the nearby Peckham Library (see pp. 88–89), yet this project is significant as a truly transformational example of reuse, reflecting the continuing growth of Southwark's artistic and design community.

Architect Ken Taylor and sculptor Julia Manheim, who are both directors in the multi-disciplinary (architecture/design/art) practice Quay 2C, acquired the building in King's Grove from Southwark Council in 1998 – planners had signified (after consultation with local residents) that change of use from light industrial to live/work accommodation was acceptable. The existing fabric was in poor condition after several years of disuse, but its 'industrial barn' aesthetic appealed to Taylor and Manheim and was something they endeavoured to retain in the reuse project. (The motive, they say, was not nostalgic "but rather to reveal, as an archaeologist might enjoy, the previous uses, transformations and wear that the building had undergone".) As far as possible, not only the basic, very solid structure of the old depot but also its textures and details were retained. Reusing old materials, of course, helped keep down the cost and reflected a commitment to sustainable development.

The essence of the project is, according to Ken Taylor, "a somewhat surreal narrative of being at the seaside while in Peckham. This introduces ideas of 'between-ness', seasonal change, popular imagery, colour, weathering, *etc.*, associated with the coast, reflected in the layered quality of the scheme." The working studios are placed to the front, with living accommodation behind. Bedrooms and bathrooms are placed at first-floor level – the old roof had to be replaced – in a series of 'beach huts', externally clad in western red cedar boarding, accessed via an internal walkway and sitting above the former cold store. Living spaces are at ground-floor level. Corrugated metal sheeting, taken from the former roof, is used extensively as a wall cladding. All internal doors (other than fire doors) are items salvaged from the site.

The second phase of the project, the construction of three flats on the street front of the site, was undertaken in 2000–02. The frontage to the street is rendered, with corten steel cladding at ground-floor level. The south wall is made of sea-green reinforced plastic (commonly used for garage doors), providing daylight to the stairs, and the roof is a wave of aluminium. This eclectic mix of materials reinforces the 'as found' and layered ethos of the first phase of the project. The housing for bins and cycles on the front of the block, clad in green oak and envisaged as a boardwalk, continues the seaside theme of the beach huts. This element is sedum-roofed, giving a green horizon for passers-by. Along the side is a metre-square window, forming the smallest art gallery in Southwark and endorsing the project's creative agenda. It is planned to cover the yard along the north side of the development in resin-bonded gravel to resemble a beach.

Eclectic, certainly, with touches that some might consider eccentric, King's Grove is the sort of development that enriches the city, visually and socially.

The mixed-use King's Grove development is a conversion–extension of a former milk depot. The bedrooms and bathrooms are placed in 'beach huts' on the roof (below).

City Hall
Off Tooley Street, SE1

Foster and Partners
1998–2002

As a symbol of London government, Foster's City Hall – the seat of the Mayor of London and the Greater London Authority (GLA) – lacks both the scale and the gravitas of the old County Hall, where the London County Council and its successor, the Greater London Council (GLC), were based for over sixty years until the latter was wound up by Margaret Thatcher.

Yet this contrast is surely deliberate: in comparison to the GLC, the GLA is a slimline organization. Not surprisingly, perhaps, in London New Labour eschewed the route taken by devolved government in Scotland and Wales, where bespoke parliamentary/assembly buildings were commissioned as a result of high-level design competitions. For London, the competition for the new City Hall was decided on commercial as much as architectural criteria, with the consortium that was developing More London (see pp. 94–95), to a Foster masterplan, triumphing over an alternative deal offered by

the developers of Victoria House in Bloomsbury, with Will Alsop as prospective architect. Neither mayor nor GLA, both yet to be elected when the deal was done in 1998, had any say over the choice of site or architect.

City Hall occupies a pivotal site in the More London development, at the termination of the pedestrian avenue leading from Tooley Street, looking across the river to the City. It is certainly a recognizable landmark, compared by Mayor Ken Livingstone (before his election) to "a glass testicle". The project overlapped with Foster's work on the Berlin Reichstag, and there are parallels between the two – in terms both of the ramp that extends through City Hall and of its low-energy environmental strategy – though the entire building could be accommodated in the Reichstag debating chamber.

The lightness and transparency promised by early impressions of the building have not been entirely realized – 75% of the exterior is

clad in solid insulated panels, with triple glazing and other solar controls reinforcing its opaque character. Internally, the ramp lacks the elegance of that in the Reichstag and, given the limited public access to City Hall, seems a slightly pointless feature – but the large reception space at the top of the building ("London's living room") has fine views over South London and Docklands. For all its imperfections, City Hall is an important landmark both physically and symbolically. The landscaping around the building, with a 1000-seat open arena spilling out from the public cafeteria, excellent paving, and all external lighting ingeniously concentrated on a single mast, is exemplary. From here, one gets a good view of a later Foster building, 30 St Mary Axe (or the 'Gherkin', as it is popularly known), in which the organic, free form of City Hall is spectacularly developed.

Externally an enigmatic landmark on the riverside, City Hall is internally dominated by a spiral ramp (opposite) that connects all spaces: a spectacular feature, if of dubious practical value.

More London Development
Off Tooley Street, SE1
Foster and Partners
1998–

A catchy title for a development that has transformed one of Southwark's most tempting (and most disputed) brownfield sites and, quite fortuitously, has given the borough the seat of the Mayor of London. City Hall (see pp. 92–93) is essentially a developer's building, leased to the mayor and the Greater London Authority and commissioned by central government before either was elected. It gives obvious cachet to what is fundamentally a very large (200,000 sq m/ 2 million sq ft) office development (though with shopping, a hotel and arts facilities attached) that underlines the reality of Southwark's challenge to the dominance of the City.

The wharves and warehouses between London Bridge and Tower Bridge (which stood on the site of Edward II's summer palace and the moated manor house of Sir John Fastolff) were closed down in the late 1960s, but large-scale development began only after 1980, when the controversial London Bridge City project got under way as a mix of (generally depressing) new blocks and radically reconstructed historic buildings. Proposals published in the late 1980s for 'London Bridge City Phase II' included a 'Venice on Thames' scheme by John Simpson, and Johnson/Burgee's bizarre paraphrase of the Palace of Westminster using reflective glazing. Fortunately, all fell victim to the recession of the early 1990s, and the 5.3 ha (13 acre) site remained fallow until construction of the Foster project, along with City Hall – all to a masterplan of 1998 – began in 2000, following a series of archaeological digs.

More London includes six large office buildings by Foster, three of which had been completed by the end of 2003, the largest of them housing the UK headquarters of accountants Ernst & Young. They are typical of the practice's recent commercial work in London: slick, efficient, scrupulously detailed and built to a well-tried formula. More significant, however, than the architecture is the masterplan, developed in association with Space Syntax Ltd. It is commercially astute in opening up the site to the river, emphasizing the connection to the City and enhancing property values. But it has also created a bold new pedestrian avenue linking London Bridge Underground station with City Hall and Tower Bridge, along with two new piazzas and a series of reopened routes between Tooley Street and the river. Parking and service roads are banished below ground. Landscaping, street furniture and public artworks are all finished to a high standard.

This is, indeed, the "high-quality, international business development" promoted by its developers. But it offers genuine benefits to the local community in terms not only of employment and regeneration but also by opening up the Thames to the hinterland of Bermondsey, and contributing substantially to London's ongoing rediscovery of its single greatest physical asset, its river. And while London Bridge City was (and remains) a gated development – recognizably private territory, closed at night – More London is open to all at all hours, a genuinely public domain.

More London contains a series of high-quality office buildings that look across the Thames towards the City (below). An integral feature of the masterplan is a central avenue (opposite) connecting London Bridge station with City Hall and Tower Bridge.

London College of Communication
St George's Road, SE1

Allies & Morrison Architects
1998–2003

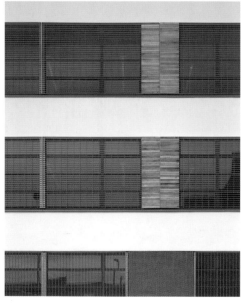

The London College of Printing (as it was previously known) occupies a complex at the Elephant & Castle constructed in two phases (1960–64 and 1969–73) to designs by the London County Council Architects' Department and its successors at the Greater London Council (GLC). These are thoroughly decent buildings that reflect the move from the International Style towards the more quirky approach that also produced the GLC's Pimlico School. After the college became part of the London Institute and was renamed, the decision was taken to relocate the media school from its site in Clerkenwell. Allies & Morrison was appointed in 1998 both to design a new building to house the school and to produce a masterplan strategy for integrating all the buildings on the site. The project was developed in the context of plans to redevelop the area around the Elephant. Planning permission was given in 2000 and construction took place in 2001–03.

The new five-storey, white-rendered media school block is placed along the residential Oswin Street, to the rear of the site. As one would expect of its architects, it makes an appropriate response to its context – a matter of "keeping in keeping". Allies & Morrison was instinctively sympathetic to the rational order of the 1960s buildings, though the addition of timber cladding panels and metal window screens (the latter giving the façades a somewhat inscrutable look) are typical twenty-first-century interventions. Internally, however, the building has a lightness of touch and generosity of scale not found in the college's earlier buildings.

The other element in the client brief – the creation of a small campus, in effect, out of a collection of buildings – generated the 'street', a toplit first-floor circulation space, 63 m (100 ft) long, that extends across the site from a new triple-height main entrance to connect the college's three blocks. The use of red-painted steel for the roof structure, emerging to form a Miesian portico on the entrance front, clearly marks the route and lifts the spirits at the same time. Refurbishment of other buildings on the site is continuing in line with the Allies & Morrison masterplan.

Allies & Morrison's project for the London College of Communication provides a physical and visual connection between existing buildings being refurbished as part of a masterplan for this prominent site.

Whiteford Studio and House
Half Moon Lane, SE24

Cullum & Nightingale Architects
1998–2004

Half Moon Lane is a leafy suburban street within the Dulwich Estate – not a natural habitat for new architecture. However, Cullum & Nightingale's studio, completed in 1999, and adjacent house, constructed from 2003 to 2004 for the artist Kate Whiteford and her husband, make a well-mannered but highly individual contribution to the local scene. On a small, awkwardly shaped site at the intersection of two roads, the architects have created a fusion of architecture and landscape, of internal and external space, which is essentially modern yet has clear roots in the Arts and Crafts tradition. There is more than a hint of Mackintosh in the house – Kate Whiteford is Scottish – and

memories, too, of Africa – Whiteford worked with Cullum & Nightingale on a major artwork for the British High Commission building in Nairobi.

The studio is a low-cost workspace – of brick with a copper-clad roof externally, one big volume internally – with a mezzanine covering a small kitchen and shower room. Two large north-facing dormer windows provide the necessary even light for painting. Studio and house enclose a small courtyard. The house forms a strong composition, with dormers on its eastern elevation connecting it visually to the studio, and a bold chimney stack with internal and external fireplaces. Constructed

of brick, partly rendered, it is roofed in copper, with copper downpipes. Inside, the emphasis is on space and light. The full-height living space, like a medieval hall, is its social heart, with subsidiary spaces opening off it, and bedrooms and bathrooms on the first floor accessed via an open gallery. A 'secret' stair, buried in the wall, connects the living room with the main bedroom above.

With plenty of conviction but an absence of needless whimsy, Cullum & Nightingale have reinterpreted the suburban tradition in a thoroughly modern manner to create a house that must be as inspirational to live in as it is engaging to look at.

Making good use of an awkward suburban site, Cullum & Nightingale's studio and house draw inspiration from Arts and Crafts roots but reinterpret them in a modern manner.

Palestra
Blackfriars Road, SE1

Alsop Architects
1999–2006

The Palestra office development, on a prominent site (formerly occupied by Orbit House, a poor-quality 1960s block) opposite Southwark Underground station (see pp. 58–59), is Will Alsop's second building in Southwark, and his first new-build commercial project in Britain.

The scheme won planning consent in 2000, but construction work on the thirteen-storey, 28,000 sq m (300,000 sq ft) building began only at the end of 2003, with completion scheduled for mid-2006. The client is Mallory Clifford of Blackfriars Investments, a company that is also working with Alsop on redevelopment plans for the Puddle Dock area of the City of London.

This is a big building, intensifying the use of the site, but its impact is softened by Alsop's innovative treatment of both form and façade. The floors are conceived as a series of horizontal boxes stacked one on top of the other and cantilevering over the street, with the ground floor cut away to provide sheltered public space animated by shops and cafés. Double-height spaces, mezzanines and terraces form interventions into the highly efficient 30 m (100 ft) wide floor spans. The glazing system was developed in collaboration with manufacturer Pilkington, and makes use of patterning baked on to the glass to achieve the rich colour and pattern that is characteristic of Alsop's architecture.

Palestra will be the first sight that countless visitors, using Southwark Jubilee line station *en route* to Tate Modern (see pp. 66–67), will see as they surface in SE1. Appropriately, it is a building where art is not applied as an extra, but is an integral part of the architecture. Alsop is known as a painter as well as an architect, but he has rarely had a canvas on this scale.

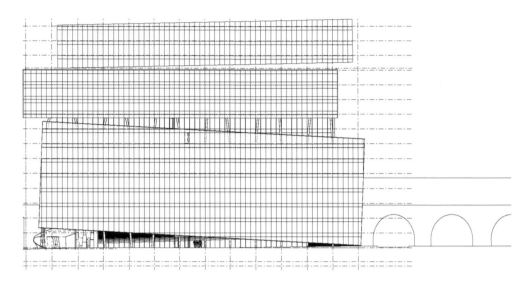

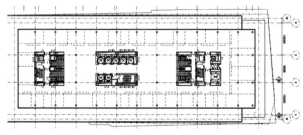

Strongly coloured and vigorously modelled, Alsop's Palestra is one of the landmark new commercial developments in Southwark reflecting the influence of Tate Modern and the Jubilee Line Extension.

Charter School
Red Post Hill, SE24

Penoyre & Prasad Architects
1999–2006

Nearly half a century ago, Chamberlin, Powell & Bon's Geoffrey Chaucer School, off the New Kent Road, was a confident symbol of the rise of comprehensive education. It remains in use today. Dulwich High School for Boys (formerly William Penn School), of similar vintage and designed by the London County Council's Schools Department, fared less well. With numbers falling to an unviable level during the 1990s, it faced closure and possible demolition, though the buildings – if lacking the human touch and in need of major refurbishment – had intrinsic merit.

Penoyre & Prasad's project, launched in 1999 after the practice won the commission in competition, has transformed the tired 1950s campus into a landmark twenty-first-century school, strongly rooted in the local community and achieving results in both academic and social terms. When the Charter School admitted its first pupils, in autumn 2000 – with the reconstruction still very much in progress – the 180 available places were oversubscribed by 500%. A roll-call of 1500 is envisaged by 2006.

The core idea of the project – developed in consultation with the head teacher, governors and local education authority – was the retention and refurbishment of the existing buildings. The rationale was essentially practical: no alternative site in the Dulwich area was available for a new school – and clearing the site and building from scratch would have greatly delayed the advent of a facility that had strong support from local parents, whose children were commuting considerable distances to school. The 1950s buildings were, in any case, structurally sound, though services needed to be renewed, accessibility issues tackled and the whole 11,000 sq m (120,000 sq ft) complex updated in line with changing approaches to schooling. And all this within a relatively modest budget – around £17 million to date. Some of the buildings have yet to be tackled, and the projected landscaping is still incomplete.

The main four-storey teaching block had to be stripped back to its structural frame to eradicate large quantities of asbestos. Externally it has been refaced using boldly coloured purple and blue cladding, and looks brand new. The landscape around the buildings has been reconfigured: the main entrance, used by all, leads into a glazed court (previously open to the elements but now an all-weather social space) with a new roof supported on steel 'trees', sculptural in their dynamism. From here, glazed corridors and covered walkways connect all the blocks, with every building accessible to all. Lift shafts, with glazed tops are, as *The Architects' Journal* commented, "beacons of renewal". This project is about transformation, but with respect for context and an appropriate regard for the resource value of existing buildings.

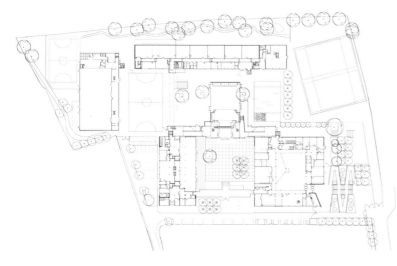

The Charter School occupies a series of 1950s buildings refurbished and connected by new public spaces (site plan, left) including the central glazed court (right).

Lord House
Grove Park, SE5

Buro Boro Architects/SE5 Architects
2000–02

Grove Park is a leafy suburban enclave in Camberwell, a place of solid Victorian villas and, almost inevitably, included in one of Southwark's conservation areas. The clients for this elegant new house, as thoroughly contemporary as it is appropriately contextual, lived in a large late nineteenth-century semi-detached house next door, but wanted to move to a smaller and more convenient house after their children left home. They acquired the garden site for their new house back in the 1980s from British Rail, but were initially advised by Southwark planners that an 'in keeping' design – a pastiche, in effect, built of brick with a pitched roof – would be required if planning consent were ever to be given.

When architects Niki Borowiecki and Liz Borowiecka came on the scene in 1996, however, insistent that the idea of a thoroughly modern house should be pursued, planners welcomed their proposals and planning permission was granted. The site has a pronounced slope down to an adjacent railway line, so that a flat platform had to be created as a base for the house, which is set 1.5 m (5 ft) below pavement level, thus preserving views from the street to the area of woodland beyond and giving the interiors an element of privacy. (In winter, the Millennium Dome and towers of Canary Wharf can be glimpsed through the trees.)

Clad in white render, the house has more than a hint of the 'White Modern' style of the 1930s. The internal focus is on a central entrance hall/dining space – rising the full height of the house, daylit from above and with full-height windows providing views out to the street and landscape – off which all the rooms open. The architects describe the plan as "a modern version of the Georgian villa" – the emphasis is on comfort and convenience rather than extreme effects. The house has been beautifully crafted, with floors of oak, slate and limestone, and much high-quality joinery. Antique furniture, pictures and lots of books, brought from the clients' old house, blend happily with the architecture. The garden has been developed in consultation with the architects. The roof of the house is planted with sedum, providing an excellent layer of insulation and ensuring that neighbours have a green outlook from their bedroom windows. Here is a project that demonstrates the potential of new design to enhance a historic and much-loved area.

A straightforward modern intervention into an established Victorian enclave, the Lord House is distinguished by its well-proportioned, beautifully lit and finely crafted interiors.

Fashion and Textile Museum

Bermondsey Street, SE1

Ricardo Legorreta/Alan Camp Architects
2000–03

An exotic intruder into historic Bermondsey, the Fashion and Textile Museum is the personal creation of the fashion designer Zandra Rhodes and the only work in Europe to date by the veteran Mexican architect Ricardo Legorreta.

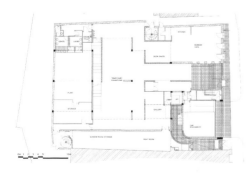

A touch of old Mexico in the hinterland of London Bridge? Ricardo Legorreta is probably Mexico's best-known living architect and he has also worked extensively in West Coast USA, but the Fashion and Textile Museum is his first building in Europe. The commission came directly from flamboyant fashion designer Zandra Rhodes, whose personal enthusiasm has driven the project – Rhodes had warmed to Legorreta's work when she was in California.

Rhodes acquired the utilitarian 1950s warehouse back in the mid-1990s, with the aim of creating a museum to house a collection of over 3000 garments plus temporary exhibitions of the work of leading designers along with an apartment and design studio for her own use. Legorreta's proposal was basically a conversion of the existing building, but the project needed an infusion of funding to make it viable and the Lottery turned it down. Local architect Alan Camp was brought in to amend the scheme in collaboration with Legorreta: a development of eight apartments was added in a new extension at the rear of the building, and their sale provided the funding to open the first phase.

The museum makes an immediate and striking impact on the Bermondsey street scene with a façade covered in terracotta-coloured render, and an entrance framed in vivid pink. A (non-functional) pink chimney punctuates the roofline. Inside, a blue and pink barrel-vaulted passage leads into the exhibition area. The generous volume of the original warehouse has been retained and skilfully exploited, with a great yellow ramp connecting the principal display spaces on the ground and mezzanine levels. The internal finishes are generally tough and industrial in feel, and often quite crude – the budget for the project was very tight – though Rhodes's exuberant taste is probably reflected in the elaborate terrazzo floor in the foyer area. It is hoped to remedy some of the recognized imperfections in future phases of work. For some, this development is vulgar and inappropriate to its context. Yet it adds an exotic element of colour and fancy to Bermondsey, which is tough enough to take it, and commands respect for its sheer eccentricity.

Unicorn Theatre for Children
Tooley Street, SE1

Keith Williams Architects
2000–05

The Unicorn Theatre for Children was founded as long ago as 1947 but has never had a home of its own. Its new premises on Tooley Street are being constructed with the help of Arts Council, Lottery and other public funding, as well as donations from private sources and charitable trusts. The project reflects the revitalization of the area around London Bridge station and Tooley Street, linked to the development of More London and the new City Hall (see pp. 94–95 and 92–93). Keith Williams Architects won the commission after a Europe-wide competition in 2000, and work began on site late in 2003, with opening scheduled for 2005.

The context to which the new theatre responds is highly varied. On the one hand there is Tooley Street, with its mix of old buildings on a historic street pattern, on the other, the glazed office pavilions of More London, with its generous new public spaces leading to the river. The aim was to create a new building that was deliberately un-precious, "rough but beautiful", in the words of the Unicorn's artistic director Tony Graham. The glazed elevation of the foyer to Tooley Street and Unicorn Passage (the pedestrian route to the river) reveals a transparent, multi-level space serving the main auditorium and the smaller studio theatre. The main theatre is externally expressed as a copper-clad mass, balancing above the foyer. A mix of materials includes glazed and engineering brick, and render – used to emphasize the sculptural composition of the building, which asserts itself boldly against the backcloth of More London. A corner tower forms a strong urban marker. External details and internal fit-out are both emphatically child-scaled.

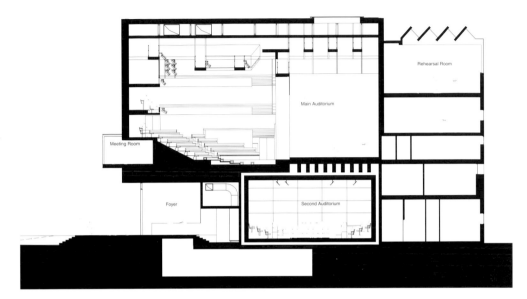

The Unicorn Theatre is part of a run of small-scale new and retained buildings that forms the southern edge of the More London development, serving to integrate it with the historic thoroughfare of Tooley Street.

Bermondsey Spa
Bermondsey, SE16

Llewellyn-Davies/Levitt Bernstein/Lifschutz Davidson/ IDOM UK and others
2000–

The Bermondsey Spa project exemplifies the new directions in regeneration that Southwark is pursuing in the first decade of the twenty-first century. Despite the renaissance of Bermondsey's riverside over the last two decades, the hinterland of the area, beyond Jamaica Road, still bears the scars of industrial decline, wartime bombing and post-war development that, while providing much-needed housing, showed little concern for any sense of place. Escaping the clean sweep that transformed other parts of the borough in the 1950s and 1960s, the Bermondsey Spa area, bisected by the viaduct of the London–Greenwich railway, survived as a patchwork of old and new, with more than its share of vacant land. The environment was poor and community facilities, including healthcare and shopping, were distinctly lacking.

The advent of the Jubilee Line Extension, with a station on Jamaica Road, vastly improved access to the area. In 2000 Southwark Council adopted a masterplan by Llewellyn-Davies for the 20 ha (50 acre) urban quarter – this envisages around 2000 new homes, along with shops, medical facilities, a 'one-stop shop' for council services and new open spaces and play areas. A considerable proportion of the land earmarked for development is owned by the council, with the rest divided among a number of owners. Southwark has sought to set a lead for other owners by launching a series of architect/ developer competitions for a number of sites, with the aim of making architectural and landscape quality a high priority.

One of the biggest players in the project is Hyde Housing Association, with a scheme for six hundred new homes, a health centre and commercial space, all designed by Levitt Bernstein, with low-energy servicing a particular feature of the scheme. Around the great Neo-classical

church of St James, Barcelona-based IDOM UK has designed a housing scheme for developer Blueprint Homes, with a 25% 'affordable' element and a nursery. Pollard Thomas Edwards is the architect for a prominent site on Grange Road that will house a new health centre (eight GP surgeries, a dentist, pharmacy and district nurse) plus seventy-four residential units for Hyde Housing Association. The 'one-stop shop' on Spa Road has been designed, by Lifschutz Davidson, as a demountable structure that can be relocated when the remainder of the adjacent site is redeveloped. Lifschutz Davidson is also the architect for the planned redevelopment of Dockley Road industrial estate to provide high-quality commercial space.

Bermondsey Spa is very much a work in progress, but it reflects Southwark's response to policy initiatives coming from central government and the Mayor of London, aimed at creating dense but attractive 'urban villages', mixed in use and social character, and based on sustainable principles. To this degree, the project provides a snapshot of the future of regeneration in the borough.

Housing designed by IDOM UK (top), mixed-use housing and commercial development by Levitt Bernstein (opposite) and a health centre on Grange Road by Pollard Thomas Edwards architects (above right) form three of the elements of the Bermondsey Spa redevelopment.

111

Elephant & Castle Masterplan
Elephant & Castle, SE1

Foster and Partners and others
(Phase 1)/MAKE (Phase 2)
2000—

The regeneration of the Elephant & Castle and its reinstatement as "a vibrant, thriving and successful new mixed-use town centre … a place where people want to live, to work and to visit for shopping and leisure" is a key component in Southwark's regeneration strategy. Indeed, the Elephant can again be what it once was: a focus of commercial, cultural and social life for a large area of south London.

The form of redevelopment that occurred after the Second World War (when the area was badly bombed) has clearly contributed to its decline, and in recent years it has suffered from a distinctly negative image. In part, this is a result of the domination of roads and traffic, with the major public transport interchange palpably inconvenient and outmoded, and circulation dependent on subterranean tunnels. But the bland architecture of the 1960s shopping centre does not help either and it is rightly earmarked for demolition. The nearby Heygate Estate is one of the least loved of Southwark's post-war housing schemes and is now scheduled for replacement.

The involvement of the local residential and business community is seen as fundamental to the project. An earlier version of the masterplan, which was seen as being dominated by retailing, was abandoned after strong local criticism. The revised Foster and Partners plan provided for up to 650,000 sq m (6,996,600 sq ft) of mixed-use development, including over 5000 new homes, shops, restaurants, cafés, offices and new public buildings including, potentially, a city academy,

leisure centre and library. The transport interchange will be substantially improved. Sustainability, in the broadest sense, is seen as a key theme in the development of detailed designs for buildings.

More important than buildings, perhaps, is the new public domain, essentially based on streets and squares at ground level. Most dramatic is the new civic square planned at the heart of the reconstructed quarter, linked to a new Walworth High Street (an extension of Walworth Road) and acting as the site for the tallest buildings in the masterplan area. Two striking residential towers will be markers of renewal. A new market square will offer shopping more akin to that of Borough Market than that of the typical high street. On the site of the Heygate Estate, a town park will be the focus of a new residential quarter.

This is a hugely ambitious project but one that can be achieved in a phased programme, via a partnership of public and private sectors, within ten to fifteen years. Its realization is vital not only for Southwark but also for London: this project epitomizes the vision of a dense, vibrant, environmentally healthy London expressed in the Urban Task Force report, and is the obverse of the continuing sprawl of the capital into the countryside. During 2004, the architectural practice MAKE was appointed masterplanner to the next phase of the development, in succession to Foster and Partners.

Artists' impressions of the Elephant & Castle by Foster and Partners, reflecting the 2003 masterplan, produced in collaboration with GEL Architects, Space Syntax and Tibbalds Urban Design.

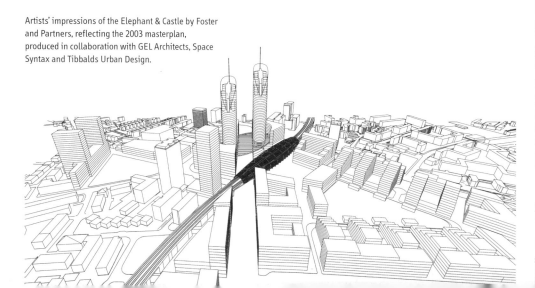

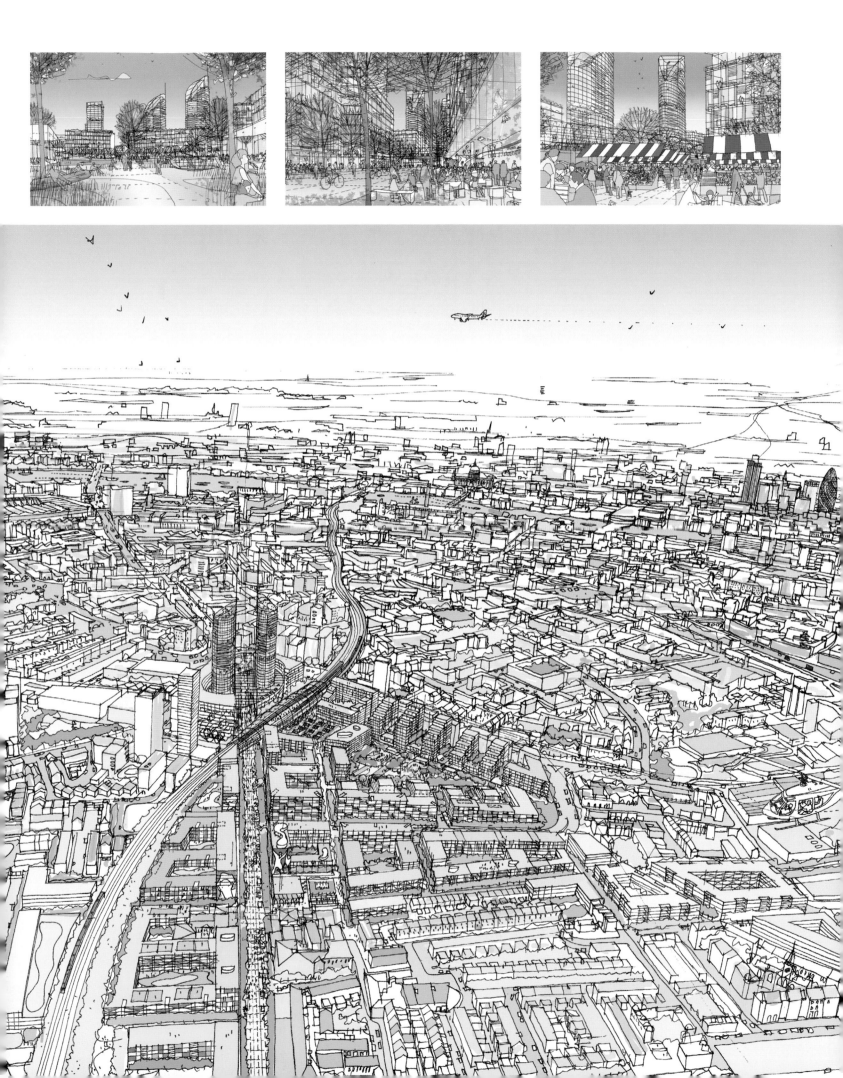

London Bridge Tower
London Bridge, SE1

Renzo Piano Building Workshop
2000–

For developer Irvine Sellar the London Bridge Tower will be a "global landmark ... a building of which Londoners can be rightly proud". For Southwark Council, which has consistently backed Sellar's vision, the project reflects Southwark's role as "a vibrant part of central London, benefiting from and contributing to London as a global city".

Initial proposals for the tower were drawn up by Broadway Malyan, but towards the end of 2000 Renzo Piano was brought in completely to rethink the scheme, intended to replace an undistinguished 1970s office tower adjacent to London Bridge station. At this stage, the eighty-seven-storey building was to be 420 m (1380 ft) high, easily the tallest habitable building in Europe. By the time of the planning submission in 2001, its height had been cut to 306 m (1016 ft) and sixty-eight storeys – and the tower reconfigured as a slim spiked form. Opposition to the project came from English Heritage (on 'strategic views' grounds). London Mayor Ken Livingstone, however, emerged as a strong supporter of the project, which also won backing from the Commission for Architecture and the Built Environment and the approval of the government following a public inquiry in 2003. With 80,000 sq m (850,000 sq ft) net of office, hotel and residential space, the tower would be a major regenerative move and a boost to the economy of Southwark. Its location over a major transport hub is in line with planning policies.

Piano conceives the slender, spire-like form of the tower – 'a shard of glass' – as a positive addition to the London skyline and believes that its presence will be far more ethereal than opponents of the scheme allege. The tower will have highly sophisticated glazing, with expressive façades of angled panes intended to reflect light and the changing patterns of the sky, so that the perceived form of the building will vary with the weather and the seasons. It will be anchored to the site by a base containing shops, restaurants, and exhibition and conference spaces – up to 7000 people could work in it. The possible shelving, at least for the present, of the proposed London Bridge station reconstruction is unfortunate in that the two projects could have been closely integrated, but improved station facilities are promised as part of the Piano scheme.

Renzo Piano's London Bridge Tower will provide a defining feature on the London skyline, and was strongly endorsed by Southwark Council against opposition from English Heritage, for its contribution to regeneration and its architectural quality.

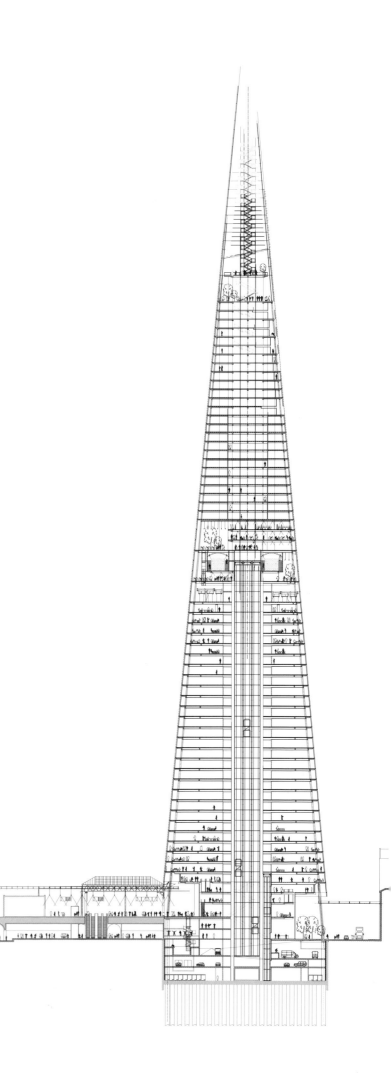

Architects' Offices
Southwark Street, SE1

Allies & Morrison Architects
2001–03

This elegant and beautifully detailed building was designed by Allies & Morrison as the growing practice's own headquarters. It currently houses around 150 staff, who moved here in 2003 from offices in the West End.

From the street, the building has a sleek and transparent look, with full-height glazing on the north elevation providing generous amounts of natural light to the studios. Pivoted sunscreens, brightly coloured, can be used to deflect sunlight when it becomes distracting, or merely to provide privacy – a simple but elegant device that is distinctly 'low-tech'. Internally, the concrete structural frame is freely exposed in fair-faced form within the offices and other areas. There are no suspended ceilings and a minimum of plasterboard. The main stair is a *tour de force* in cast concrete. A highly disciplined approach to the use of materials was pursued throughout: metalwork is finished to a heavy-duty industrial grade, and floors are covered in black granite or grey resin. A welded metal stair connects the reception area with the studios above and the basement area, used for workshops and support spaces. Colour is used sparingly, but to good effect.

To the rear, the building has an irregular footprint and a stepped form, deferring to established rights of light. A triple-height atrium visually connects all of the studio spaces, creating a sense of connectivity within the six storeys of accommodation. A roof garden, looking south and concealed from the street, is an attractive staff amenity. The intention is to develop the ground floor as a gallery and display/social space – and a new public passageway, part of a pedestrian route from the river through the Bankside 123 development (also designed by Allies & Morrison – see pp. 118–19) into the hinterland of Southwark Street, runs through the building at this level.

Allies & Morrison has enhanced Southwark Street – which can seem a monotonous thoroughfare – with its new offices. On a dark winter afternoon, the view into the offices from the street is a visual delight – they must be even more delightful to use.

Externally highly transparent, the interior spaces of Allies & Morrison's practice offices are designed to encourage communication and interaction, and are meticulously finished.

Bankside 123
Southwark Street, SE1

Allies & Morrison Architects
2001–05

St Christopher's House, which this development replaces, was allegedly "the largest office block under one roof in Europe" when completed in 1959. Its blank mass, 625 m (228 ft) long, formed a depressing presence on Southwark Street, filling a site that before the Second World War had been a fine-grained mix of housing and small industrial buildings.

St Christopher's House was demolished in 2003. Allies & Morrison's project, for Land Securities, significantly increases the amount of office space on the site, while providing much-needed new shopping for the area, and – most significantly – creating public routes across the site to and from Tate Modern (see pp. 66–67).

The three new buildings, containing more than 100,000 sq m (1.1 million sq ft) gross of office space and 9300 sq m (100,000 sq ft) of retailing, cafés and bars at street level, are arranged as city blocks penetrated by two pedestrian routes through the site, with two new public spaces at their eastern and western ends. The aim is to create a lively 'high street' frontage to Southwark Street, with shops and cafés opening off wide, tree-lined pavements. The buildings are conceived as a group, but each is given a distinctive identity by the use of a wide palette of materials – metal and glass, terracotta and precast concrete. In contrast to the monolithic uniformity of St Christopher's House, the new blocks are carefully massed in response to their context, with the scale of the scheme diminishing from west to east (where it abuts an area of housing).

Land Securities, as developer, is committed to the belief that "the quality of the public realm is fundamental to the success of the scheme". It is the permeability of the reconfigured site, and the quality of its new landscape, that will attract users – with its amenities reinforcing the appeal of the offices to prestigious clients. The future expansion of Tate Modern into the southern half of the former Bankside Power Station is likely to further enhance the attractions of the site.

Replacing a dismal 1950s building, Bankside 123 combines office space with shops and restaurants to create a new mixed-use quarter adjacent to Tate Modern.

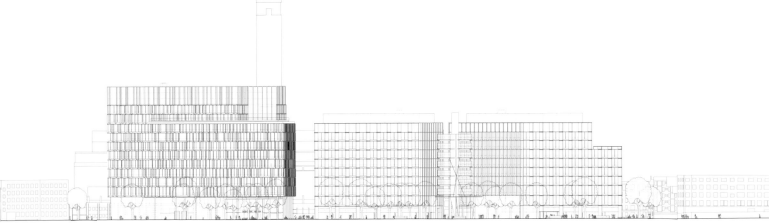

Bermondsey Wall West
Bermondsey Wall, SE1

Glen Howells Architects
2001—

Wartime bombing and post-war clearances destroyed the nineteenth-century warehouses that created a townscape here as dramatic as that of Shad Thames. Glenn Howells's eight-storey mixed-use development (forty-seven apartments, with commercial use on the ground floor) puts a distinctively contemporary stamp on this stretch of riverside.

Prominently sited – it can be seen from Tower Bridge – the scheme is notable for the sheer elegance of its form and detailing, and for its appropriate scale, setting a precedent, perhaps, for future development in the vicinity. The building fills its site hard up to the pavement, in line with neighbouring structures, but is set back 4 m (13 ft) at ground level on the north to accommodate the river walkway. The development of a restaurant at this level is planned, animating the riverfront and extending into a covered external area.

The strong expression of the structural frame, clad in clear and translucent glass, is typical of the Birmingham-based architect; it is a highly disciplined composition that eschews needless display in favour of an orderly expression of the internal plan. In this respect, at least, the building draws on the precedent of the 'functional tradition' of warehouse design.

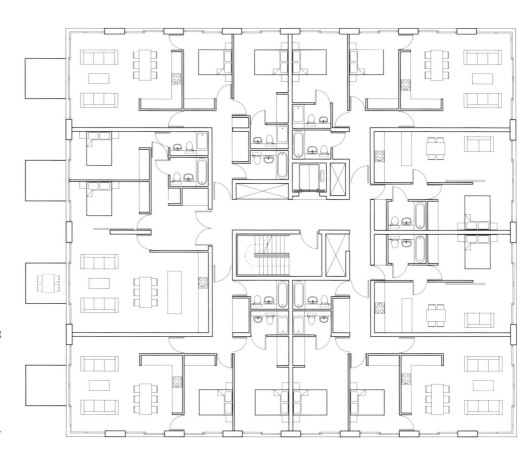

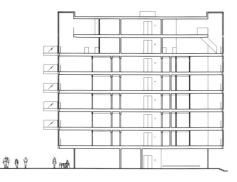

Infilling a derelict site on the riverside, Glen Howell's Bermondsey Wall West project has a strong discipline lacking in some earlier residential projects in the area.

Bermondsey Square
Bermondsey Square, SE1
Munkenbeck & Marshall
2002—

This project has had a long period of planning and design: Munkenbeck & Marshall was brought in only in 2002, after a project of 1998 by another practice was finally abandoned. A start on site is planned for November 2004.

The site is south of Tower Bridge, framed by Tower Bridge Road, Abbey Street and Bermondsey Street, and below it are the remains of the lost Bermondsey Abbey. It has long been owned by Southwark Council, which formed a joint venture with developer Urban Catalyst to progress this regenerative project – it exemplifies the way in which the tide of development along the river is now extending inland.

This is a genuine mixed-use project, with housing (private and 'affordable'), offices, shops and a restaurant, a cinema and a ninety-room 'boutique' hotel included. At its heart is a new public square, intended for market use – an antiques market is already established on the site. Architect Steve Marshall envisages it as "an urban salon … a vast outdoor room", which will be managed as a multi-purpose community resource. The buildings around the square are simple in terms of construction, with timber and monoflex cladding – the latter an innovation 'lifted' from the technology of advertising panels – on a steel frame. The intention is to change the monoflex panels four times annually, each refit featuring a different artwork, so that the square "reinvents itself" regularly. The idea is in tune with the developing identity of Bermondsey Street as a haunt of artists, with a number of galleries already established there. Giant chandeliers, rather than conventional street lights, will illuminate the square by night.

Working with services engineer Atelier 10, the architects envisage Bermondsey Square as a model of low-energy development. There are proposals to generate heat and power on site, and to provide a "smart car club", with plug points adjacent to the square. If the ambitious agenda of this project is realized, it will truly form a pointer to the high-density, sustainable urban housing that is vital to the long-term future of London as an inhabitable city.

The mixed-use Bermondsey Square project is conceived as an outdoor room, illuminated by giant chandeliers (opposite), and is intended as a model of sustainability.

Mixed-use Development
Clink Street/Stoney Street, SE1
Edward Cullinan Architects
2003–

Clink Street today epitomizes the renewal of Southwark's riverside, a much-frequented stretch of the tourist route connecting London Bridge, Southwark Cathedral, Borough Market, the Globe and Tate Modern. It has plenty of Docklands atmosphere, though the monumental warehouses – notably St Mary Overie's Wharf – that survived here into the 1980s have gone. The dominant presence today is the large bank headquarters that frames two sides of Winchester Square. Like many Postmodernist schemes of its period, it was full of good intentions – its architecture clearly aims to evoke the warehouse aesthetic – but the effect is ponderous, and its blank office elevations do nothing for the street.

Winchester Square marks the site of the central court of the medieval palace of the Bishops of Winchester. Today it is a forlorn spot – used for parking, and enclosed to the west by a utilitarian warehouse block of the 1960s. The lost splendour of the palace is represented by just one remarkable fragment: a fine fourteenth-century rose window, discovered after a warehouse fire in the mid-nineteenth century and visible from Clink Street. This is currently prefaced by a sunken gravel-covered area of no practical use, which has become a trap for litter.

The memory of Winchester Palace is the starting-point for Edward Cullinan Architects's mixed-use project: an exercise in contextual Modernism, which draws on nearby Borough Market and the great brick railway viaducts that are defining features of the surrounding area. The scheme mixes residential (fourteen apartments), office and retail uses in a series of distinct blocks along Clink Street, Stoney Street and Winchester Walk. Winchester Square becomes a lively public space, with offices over shops and restaurants, accessible from all sides. A small new piazza is formed at the junction of Clink Street and Stoney Street, providing a place where the famous rose window can be seen properly. The architecture of the scheme is a disciplined reinterpretation of what used to be called "the functional tradition of industrial design", using brick and timber to reinforce the tightly enclosed character of the streetscape. Timbers from a (much-altered) Victorian industrial building on Winchester Walk will be reused elsewhere. A Victorian smithy at the junction of Winchester Walk and Stoney Street is retained and incorporated into the new development, which is being promoted by the long-term owners of the site.

This project is about reinforcing continuities – of ownership, memory and built form – in an area where (with the very important exception of Borough Market) the uses that prevailed until very recently have vanished. It promises to generate architecture that is exceptional and entirely contemporary, while deferring to context in a creative fashion.

Edward Cullinan's project on Clink Street/Stoney Street follows the footprint of Winchester Palace, replacing a dismal 1960s warehouse and recreating the historic Winchester Square as a public space.

Further Reading

Picture Credits

Peter Ackroyd, *London: The Biography*, London (Chatto & Windus) 2000

R.J.M. Carr (ed.), *Dockland: An Illustrated Historical Survey of Life and Work in East London*, London (GLC) 1986

Tim Charlesworth, *Architecture of Peckham*, London (Chener Books) 1988

Bridget Cherry and Nikolaus Pevsner, *The Buildings of England, London 2: South*, New Haven CT and London (Yale University Press) 2002

H.J. Dyos, *Victorian Suburb: A Study of the Growth of Camberwell*, Leicester (Leicester University Press) 1961

Samantha Hardingham, *London: A Guide to Recent Architecture*, 6th edn, London (B.T. Batsford) 2003

Hermione Hobhouse, *Lost London*, London (Macmillan) 1971

Edward Jones and Christopher Woodward, *A Guide to the Architecture of London*, 2nd edn, London (W.W. Norton & Co) 1992

Charles E. Lee, *Sixty Years of the Northern Line*, London (London Transport) 1967

Kenneth Powell (ed.), *World Cities: London*, London (Academy Editions) 1993

Kenneth Powell, *The Jubilee Line Extension*, London (Laurence King Publishing) 2000

Kenneth Powell, *New London Architecture*, London (Merrell) 2001

Karl Sabbagh, *Power into Art: Creating the Tate Modern, Bankside*, London (Penguin Books) 2001

John Schofield, *The Building of London: From the Conquest to the Great Fire*, 3rd edn, Stroud (Sutton Publishing) 1999

Muriel Spark, *The Ballad of Peckham Rye*, London (Macmillan) 1960

Deyan Sudjic, Peter Cook and Jonathan Meades, *English Extremists: The Architecture of Campbell Zogolovitch Wilkinson Gough*, London (Fourth Estate) 1988

Richard Tames, *Southwark Past*, London (Historical Publications) 2001

Giles Waterfield (ed.), *Soane and After: The Architecture of Dulwich Picture Gallery*, London (Dulwich Picture Gallery) 1987

Ben Weinreb and Christopher Hibbert (eds.), *The London Encyclopaedia*, London (Papermac) 1993

Stephanie Williams, *Docklands*, ADT Architecture Guide, London (Architecture, Design and Technology) 1990

Elizabeth Williamson and Nikolaus Pevsner, *The Buildings of England: London Docklands*, London (Penguin Books) 1998

Index